Real Estate

EVERRYTHING YOU NEED TO KNOW

E. VEAZIE GILMORE

November 1, 2019

Basics of Real Estate

Property constitutes possession consisting of land and the buildings that reside on it, together with this may include oil, minerals or food. Possessions that reside on the land may be of interest to the world. This will attract investors from various real estate organizations like Century 21. Likewise, the job of an investor involves the process of purchasing, selling, or building. It is the legitimate term applied to various jurisdictions that originate from real estate property laws including lands in Africa, India, the UK, United States, Canada, Australia, and New Zealand. Corporate property is the real estate where business activities of the organization that owns or rents and manages property incidentals as well as operations are related to its primary real estate. Corporate properties may be contrasted with commercial properties, whereas the purpose of commercial property is to make a return while the purpose of the corporate property is to help the enterprise.

Commercial property

Commercial real estate is property solely for the purpose of business that offers workspace rather than residential housing. Most frequently, commercial properties are rented to clients to perform business duties. Categories of real estate properties range from one single gas station to a large shopping center. Commercial properties include retailers of all sorts, including businesses such as hotels, strip malls, restaurants, convenience shops and theme parks. The primary sections of real estate properties are residential, real estate for trade, and business commerce real estate (Chen, 2019). The residential aspect concentrates on the purchasing and selling of land for the use of housing or non-commercial purposes. The commercial sector consists of properties used for business purposes; common cases include marketing and geographical trade. Business property is comprised of attributes used for manufacturing and industrial purposes like work factories and chemical plants.

Trade property is real estate that is typically rented out for commercial or retail purposes. Investing in trade property requires the acquisition and improvement of design attributes that have been designed with the intention of housing professional clients. Unlike the residential real estate investor, commercial property investors contract out and take rent from those that occupy a workspace, rather than from residential clients. It should also be noted that land is bought for the growth of any real estate property. Continue reading to learn more about commercial and residential property.

In real estate, investing in residential properties is much more advantageous than investing in commercial properties. For most property investors, particularly for beginners, residential property investment is much simpler and easier to learn. It requires a lot of time reading content to learn about the commercial property industry and how it works. Additionally, trade property investments are riskier than a residential property that may include market stability, economics or finance, property vacancies, and the process of purchasing real estate properties.

Property investors also have the power to determine the trade of property or residential real estate values. When investing in the latter, there are some other types of residential finance options to consider. These include single-family and multi-family houses, condominiums, townhomes or duplexes. Another option is to invest in conventional real estate or what is known as Airbnb properties. Financing real estate property is a first concern for property investors, whether in the commercial or residential property industry. Nevertheless, funding for these residential properties is not difficult. There are many methods to finance real estate investments including the traditional mortgage, personal loans, earnings, savings accounts, construction loans and business partnerships with other property investors. Typical residential real estate may put an investor in a 15 or 30-year debt with a 20 percent down payment.

Businesses that compare investments of trade property or residential properties, if done correctly, should be mostly risk-free! For property investors who are not keen on taking risks should also seek to ensure the higher rate of returns on the investment of residential property and investment does the most sense. Property investing in the real estate industry has fewer risks than stock investments, particularly when investing in property for the long term. The more real estate investors spend money in properties the risks of failure or rate of success may increase because of experience. Additionally, property assets can usually have increased value because the value of property investments can increase anytime (Chen, 2019). Moreover, increased investments can mean lesser encountered risks.

In summary, real estate finance has fewer risks than other types of investments, especially when real estate property is invested in for the long term. Because real estate property finance includes tangible assets, it will always hold its value.

Cash funds, in contrast, is an intangible asset in that it is expendable from the time it is received and any time thereafter. Investors should also consider real estate broker issues. The real estate investor must determine whether he/she wants to sell the real estate property with or without the assistance of a property broker. Some choose to place a real estate property on the market through property experts who usually advise investors to hire a broker when both selling and buying real estate properties.

In real estate, there are several types of property finance options to choose from. When real estate investors buy a condominium, a townhouse, or a like-kind of property, investments should include little deposits and obligations such as those fees from a community's homeowner's association (HOA) where monthly or annual fees are paid. What exactly is a homeowner's union and what should the real estate investor learn before joining?

Homeowners associations often have limitations on how it hires employees. For instance, the real estate investor looks to rent or sell properties that might require HOA approval. Some homeowners' associations provide only 15 percent of its members with real estate services while the remainder must occupy and operate the properties as sole proprietors. Further

HOA limitations make it difficult for all real estate investors to capitalize on the properties that are sold.

Real estate investors look for finance properties that are expected to share at least a couple of attributes that are part of homeowners' associations (HOA). Some real estate investors see homeowners' unions to more limitations and monthly fees (Chen, 2019). Nevertheless, HOAs are not as bad as they are often depicted, and there are as many advantages as there are disadvantages. If the property investor is behind on his/her homeowners' association fees, the homeowner's union may be able to place a lien on some real estate properties. Additionally, if the property investor decides to defend the owner's position in court, he/she would more likely be protected. These measures may occur in rare instances, yet it is something for real estate investors to consider.

For some real estate investors, having the means to make any investment sounds unrealistic. Others may be unsure as to whether to purchase property, join the HOA group and consider the next listing. Pros and cons of homeowner's affiliations helps establish HOA rules primarily to ensure the community adheres to guidelines that include landscapes for lawns and other restrictions on outdoor appearances of real estate properties. For instance, some properties hold its value based on location that may make it seem less restrictive. Two types of properties stand out in business and residential real estate. For example, Mash Visor concentrates on providing residential property investors with listings of the best single-family houses including condominiums from urban towns throughout the globe.

Urban real estate property includes steady, low-risk residential property. In a city at upwards of $110,000 starting price for a residence with three bedrooms, compared to the average cost to buy a house, it is 41.8 percent lower. The inexpensive property investment is the world in the city's residential property industry. Together with reduced house costs, rent costs here are higher than in some of the costlier construction markets across America.

Another important benefit of putting in residential attributes is that the residential property investor is entitled to tax breaks for property reduction, property protection, repair repairs, travel expenses, legal fees, and investment property taxes. This administration also provides lower taxation rates for those investing in long-term property investments. These property tax rewards are a huge incentive for some property investors to get residential properties. The means of getting money at property brings some benefits for the residential property investor. Firstly, the resident is compelled to pay the `` alternative money fee s", which is non-refundable. The interest provides residential properties investors to make a profit when the tenant first moves in the finance place. Additionally, it gives them some protection if that statement is broken or buyers change their minds.

Another reason why residential property investment is the best way to get money is that it provides property investors to get the profit through understanding. Real property appreciation is the change in the investment place's worth over time. As a summary, residential finance attributes tend to appreciate at a higher and faster pace than other types of finance. Thanks to appreciation, the real estate investor will get the investment place, take it for 5–10 years, and then sell it for much more than the first purchase cost! The property investor has the power to achieve constant income, profit from property appreciation, and take the different property investment portfolio all without the hassle of buying an investment property and the ongoing responsibilities of being a property owner! In the section, we talk about four other investment strategies for you to invest in a property that does not require immediate property ownership or purchasing an investment property.

One important decision that property investors must do is their investment strategy (or property scheme): Invest in conventional property attributes (long-term leases) or Airbnb real estate properties (short-term rentals). While some investment properties are just appropriate for conventional property investment and others for Airbnb property investment, the most lucrative investments in property are those suitable for both! At property investment, property investors will spend for the long-term (traditional) or the short-term. One of the good things about investing in multi-house rentals is that property investors are not restricted to just one property scheme; they may decide either (Chen, 2019)! For instance, one property investor may purchase the multi-house property place and lease it out for the long-term resident (which is the most general way); while another real estate, investor might buy a multifamily rental property to rent its residential units as Airbnb rentals

It is usually best for the real estate investor to employ a real estate agent when selling or purchasing the rental place. This is particularly true if the property investor is searching for cheap property properties below market value. Property agents are masters in the property investing industry and they know where to get the best positive cash flowing investment properties for the affordable cost. Not just this, but they will be a good source to get off-market investment properties.

Agents are masters who have been in the property industry for some time. Therefore, they will be of good assistance to the real estate investor selling property finance properties. They learn how to conduct the real estate industry analysis, how to make the terms of the good sale, how to promote the investment properties, and how to make prospective buyers and close the transaction. Showing properties to potential tenants or buyers is the primary function of the property marketing Associate, also called the property-marketing representative. When working with tenants and purchasers, the property sales Associate can reveal properties, discuss transactions and makeup sales agreements. Property marketing Associates will also be for sellers. In this part, they would meet with vendors to talk about selling value, propose repairs and renovations that would help change the value of the place and make a list for the property.

Property agents are professionals who have existed in the property industry for a long time. As a result, they learn the ins and outs of the property industry and can ensure that you get the greatest income place. Not just that, real estate agents can conduct the property market investigation to get the best position, decide the best rental strategy, and help property investors take the loan for buying an investment property. In short, the real estate agent would get through the process of purchasing an investment property for you, which is good for the beginner property investor. Property brokers are masters who have been in the finance business for a period. They learn how to make the best deals and how to discuss the purchase value of the finance place. Agents can also do the property industry analysis for you! The beginner property investor can learn a lot from the agent about getting started in property investment.

If you are an authorized capitalist, you will invest in property crowdfunding. Property crowdfunding is the middle ground of active and inactive property assets (Wikipedia.org, 2019). It is dynamic in the meaning that these investors decide on the place they put in, rather than having the corporation dictate that place. Besides that, it is passive in some respects. For example, the investor may spend smaller quantities, say, $ 5,000, and even higher returns. Likewise, this capitalist is not in charge of administration and rent collection. Crowdfunding offers a good and productive choice on how to get money in real estate passively.

Property investment is the best way to spend money. End. Whether its $ 10,000 or $ 100,000, through realty investment or passive property investment, there are so many benefits to growing into a property investor. Here are three reasons that give the property the best choice to spend $ 10,000: As the minor investor, you want something that offers a better return on investment with very little risk. While there is some danger to traditional property investment, it is just not as dangerous as other types of currency assets. Look at the property industry. Which kind of place is good for you: A positively geared investment property or a positive income place? This response differs from real estate investors to property investors, dependent on the investment scheme. Some property investors choose the positively geared property but because giving money at the property before taxes is preferable than losing money on the positive income property and owning to claim it back.

One of the best options for beginner property investors in the city property industry is the turnkey investment place. Property investors will buy a positive income property from the turnkey investment property company that is relatively inexpensive ($ 80,000- $ 100,000). This sort of investment place is also important for property investors who need reliable property investment and stable rental income. Even though single-family and multi-family finance properties represent the greatest long-term investments in property, as the real estate investor you should not get out and purchase the initial finance property that comes your way! The real estate investor must perform a property industry investigation to decide whether the investment place is worth his/her money before making the purchase.

Property investors have the choice of not giving closing prices. They would get to pay their investment property with the no-closing-cost mortgage. The sort of mortgage does it so that the property investor will pay the property investment with less money upfront. While this is good, it is just felt short term. Investing is the tool that the property investor can have to create a portfolio of assets attributes. Having the mortgage for purchasing real estate property finance makes property investors leverage to invest in more investment properties with less money down! Let us take one example for a more statement: Most mortgage loans involve this property investor to move out 20 percent of the property's purchase cost as out payment, while the bank (or mortgage broker) finances the other 80%. Let us say you move 20 percent down for the acquisition of the $ 100,000 property assets.

There are numerous alternatives available for funding investment properties. The real estate investor would purchase the rental place all in cash or bring out the debt. Real estate loans range from mortgage loans (the most common form), personal currency loans, bad currency loans, and owner-occupied loans. Before having started at property investment, educate yourself on what is needed to get loans. The earlier field of focus for Drone Base in on property and property related enterprise sections, including commercial property, residential real estate, property business and growth, real property insurance and the like. I have without doubt that nearly every part of the property built, inventoried, supervised, leased, traded or surveyed (whether residential or technical) in this future few years will have an aerial image taken via drone as a core part of its profile or dossier.

Real Estate for Investors

Giving money at a property is the goal of every property investor. What most beginner property investors might expect to be an impossible destination is the rental place that pays for itself and gives some money for the investor. However, if the real estate investor realizes what the positively geared place is, then such a rental place can no longer be inaccessible. Which kind of place is good for you: A positively geared investment property or a positive income place? This response differs from real estate investors to the property investor, dependent on the investment scheme. Some property investors choose the positively geared property but because giving money at the property before taxes is preferable than losing money on the positive income property and owning to claim it back.

In the property industry, being a property investor is not the only available business or business way. If you do not believe that growing into the property investor is a good option for you, do not worry! There are numerous different choices worth exploring, one of which is growing into a property developer. So, what is the property developer? In the journal, we can answer the question, in addition to providing you with seven of the features that you want to accomplish as an investment properties creator The greatest thing about property investing is that it offers place investors with a plethora of options. A property investor may select from various types of finance properties, putting strategies, and financing methods. Under types of finance properties, one choice for property investors is multi-house property properties. These attributes may be a profitable investment, but only like any other finance; they have their advantages and disadvantages. So, if you are interested in purchasing a multi-house investment place, take a moment to read the pieces

Financing the investment place is a large concern for property investors, whether in the commercial or residential property industry. Nevertheless, gaining funding for these residential properties is not that difficult. There are many methods for finance including the traditional mortgage, personal moneylenders, hard money, line of payment, establishing partnerships with other property investors, and more! Typically, you may make a 15 or 30-year debt with 20 percent down payment in the property sector, investing in residential properties is often more advantageous than investing in technical properties. For most property investors (particularly beginners), residential property investment is much simpler and easier to see. It takes a lot of time and content to see the technical property industry and how it works. Additionally, trade property investments are riskier than residential properties involving stability, finance, vacancies, and the process of dealing and purchasing residential properties.

Furthermore, property management also needs the property investor to keep track of repairs, preserve that rental property, and deal with any issue's tenants may take. As a property investor, if you do not get the time and energy needed for property management, so property investment is likely not the best business choice for you would Typically, the business property organization would function as a rational person in a specific business. They control the rental property administration while taking on the unlimited liability of the property assets. Property investors who join the small business finance the investment place. In turn, they get passive income in the form of income from the finance place's

The first cause that does purchase and takes property the most common finance strategy is the constant income and passive income, which these rental properties offer, to property investors. When the property investor holds the investment property and leases it out to long-term tenants, he/she can take monthly rent, which serves as a stable income. Short-term income gets in this form of monthly rent gathered from renters (passive income). To get money from the purchase and take real estate property properties on the long term, the property investor only carries this finance place until it appreciates and so sells it for a higher price than the initial purchase price.t

The second benefit of putting in rent to personal households is that within this set period, property investors have the rental income in the form of the monthly rent collected from the tenant. This quantity of monthly rent is determined at this alternative property, which is better for the property investor as it allows him/her to anticipate his/her income and project his/her finances ahead before selling the investment property. Additionally, monthly rent for rent to personal houses is somewhat higher than for normal rental properties. For the property investor, the acts as compensation for getting the property investment property off the industries When investing in rent to personal houses, the choice money fee is beneficial to that both property investors and the tenants of the finance place. To the property investor, the interest allows him/her to get the profit when the tenant first moves in the rental place! Additionally, since that is the non-refundable interest, renters cannot legally ask for payment if they decide not to purchase the rental properties

Purchasing the rental place would turn the property investor up to greater tax rewards that he/she cannot make with REIT investment. Having the rental property allows the property investor to take tax deductibles for the expenses of rental property management and repair. Property investors may also take a deduction on their taxes, something they may not do with REIT dividends. Typically, property investors oversee extending taxes and protection prices as they are even the owners of the rental place. Still, the real estate investor is permitted to add in this contract that tenants of rent to personal houses are in charge of keeping the property investment property and giving for any repairs such as mowing the lawn, Raking those leaves, and cleansing out these gutters. Tenants of rent to personal houses normally take better care of the rental place. After all, it is finally going to take their coming house! That is good for property investors because they will recoup some of their expenses'

The purpose of every property investor is to get money and increase profits. At conventional property investment, rental property investors get money through the monthly rent, which they take from their tenants. Today, no matter how lucrative the rental place maybe, you will not be making a profit if you cannot get tenants to lease the finance place. That is why the first element that determines the greatest places to spend in property is the housing industry's populations the purpose of every property investor is to get wealth. Place investors get money from the monthly rent, which they take from their renters. So, no matter how great the income place is, it becomes irrelevant if renters do not invade it. Therefore, the first element to keep the eye on is occupancy rates in the property industry. The best place to get investment property has higher occupancy rates and reduced vacancy rates, meaning that income place can be busy and make a profit for the property investor's

Real estate investment does not stop after purchasing the investment place. The next step to how to spend in place is organization! The administration is key to successful property investment. As a property investor, you must get the good tenants for the income property, take monthly rent, and keep track of repairs and preserving this place. Managing the rental place is not an easy task and involves both time and effort. However, do not let that deter you as with time and experience, managing property assets properties turns into the second world to property investors.t

The buy-and-hold finance strategy runs as follows: The property investor buys the investment property, leases it out to the long-term resident, and gets money from collecting monthly rent. The good thing about getting money in property from buy-and-hold investment properties is that they make a constant income AND understand over time. What the means is that the amount of the rental place gains over time. Therefore, the property investor will make the profit by selling the buy-and-hold rental property in the time for a higher cost than the first investment. Options for beginner property investors in the city property industry is the turnkey investment place. Property investors will buy a positive income property from the turnkey investment property company that is relatively inexpensive ($ 80,000- $ 100,000). This sort of investment place is also important for property investors who need reliable property investment and stable rental income.

It will be difficult for a property investor, particularly the novice looking to get the investment place, to know exactly where to begin investing in property. At least property investors will be convinced of one thing after reading the post: Phoenix property is the great choice for property investors for 2018. The desert, warm soil, and unbearably warm weather. Then did some property investors in the time. Phoenix is a prosperous, modern city with property investments waiting to be seized. The Phoenix property industry is no longer concentrated but on retirement houses and condominiums. The desert, warm soil, and unbearably warm weather. Then did some property investors in the time. Phoenix is a prosperous, modern city with property investments waiting to be seized. The Phoenix property industry is no longer concentrated but on retirement houses and condominiums. Get the idea behind as an alternative you will miss out on some good real estate investment opportunities in Phoenix finance properties!

If you are the property investor overwhelmed by all these choices in the US housing industry for 2018, remember that Phoenix property is one viable choice for the next real estate investment. The efficiency and business development would help trade property, too as residential property investment. Phoenix investors have numerous choices for property investment strategies in Phoenix, too, with no harsh limitations on Airbnb Phoenix. Turn into a Phoenix investor in 15 hours using Mash visor and make making money at the property. Then, whether you are a beginner property investor looking to purchase your first finance property, or an experienced property investor looking for the future investment place to become your real estate investment portfolio, you should think to put in the Las Vegas property industry. At the guide, we are going to mention what makes Las Vegas the hottest property industry to put in. Furthermore, we will suggest 10 of the best neighborhoods in the Las Vegas real estate industry at which property investors should consider purchasing the finance place, as estimated by the mash visor's investment property calculator.

At the guide, we are going to mention what makes Las Vegas the hottest property industry to put in. Furthermore, we will suggest 10 of the best neighborhoods in the Las Vegas real estate industry at which property investors should consider purchasing the finance place, as estimated by the mash visor's investment property calculator. Are you a property investor looking for the future property investment place? Take investing in the Anaheim property industry! 2017 was a great year for Anaheim property investors and, from our information, it looks like the trend will remain in 2018. In the guide, we dive into what makes the Anaheim property industry a better location for purchasing property assets properties— particularly in Airbnb investment properties.

Are you a property investor looking for the investment place? We've had you hidden. Mashvisor's place Finder offers current and future Property investors with the power to search for and discover the best Property attributes of any kind (single-family homes, multi-family houses, condos, townhomes, And Airbnb leases) in the US marketplace with the click of the button. Put up with Mashvisor and begin the property investment business successfully. Instead, successful property investors make use of the mashvisor's finance property computer! Both beginner and experienced property investors can find the property investing way. It allows property investors to search for and analyze property finance properties across the US housing industry to make the most lucrative people. Not only does mashvisor's finance place calculator help you make the greatest long-term investments, but it also supports you with a place and community analysis involving cap charge, payment on cash return, positive cash flow, and more!

Managing the multi-household property place is not easy. Place management involves time, effort, organization, and attention to information which not some Property investors have. Furthermore, as a property investor, you're in charge of numerous jobs, e.g., collecting monthly rent, preserving the place, dealing with complaints, getting and evicting tenants, etc. Again, not every real estate investor will manage these obligations. In real estate finance, the property investment provides property investors with a constant flow of income in the form of the monthly rent collected from renters. Income is the profit that places investors do after estimating the variation between their monthly property income and monthly expenses of their income attributes. With property investment, the income will be monthly or quarterly depending on the form of property assets. This implies a constant income when growing into a property investor. Typically, as a passive investor, all the income gets into the pocket. When the property investor chooses to trade, property appreciation will have accumulated value for the investment property and the return on investment would be in the manner, too.

One significant real estate investment decision that property investors must do when purchasing the income place is the rental strategy they're starting to take. In real estate investment, the property investor will rent the investment place for the long-term (traditional) or the short-term (Airbnb). Which rental scheme works the greatest? The statement depends on several factors, e.g., the variety of the rental place, its size, its position, and the rental income each scheme yields. That is where the payment on cash take computer comes in. Then, whether you're a beginner property investor looking to purchase your first finance place, or an experienced property investor looking for the future income place, stay smart and make use of mashvisor's rental property calculator! The property investing tool can ensure that you make the best investment decisions and make productive finance properties in any state, city, and community in the US housing industry!

To turn into a successful property investor, you should constantly choose the best deals. The reality of property investment is huge with many investment properties types and investment strategies. The property investor may choose between rental properties, buy-and-hold, fix-and-flips, wholesaling, commercial property investment, etc. Each form and scheme have its benefits; nevertheless, property experts agree that the key to successful property investing is investing in multi-house rentals. Some property investors are attracted to the investment strategy but because buying assets property and property control are not needed. Therefore, the property investor would be able to get the profit from property investing without overseeing any repairing expenditures, mortgage payments, or supervising an investment property. Keep in mind, however, that wholesaling is still a dangerous investment, which involves education in property and business and negotiation skills, also as the relation to the network of potential buyers.

Even though single-family and multi-family finance properties represent the greatest long-term investments in real estate, as the property investor you should not get out and purchase the initial finance property that comes your way! The real estate investor must perform a property industry investigation to decide whether the investment place is worth his/her money before making the purchase.

It is always best for the property investor to employ a real estate agent when selling or purchasing the rental place. This is particularly true if the property investor is searching for cheap property properties below market value. Real estate brokers are masters in the property investing industry and they know where to get the best positive cash flowing investment properties for the affordable cost. Not just this, but they will be a good source to get off-market investment properties. While these matters would move you on the right way to avoid losing money at a property, why not talk to different property investors or even the property agent or two? Property investors and brokers will be the greatest sources of real-life knowledge about the world of property investment. They will communicate their experiences about getting money and still losing money in property. More than likely, they would be pleased to go on some good to the newcomer and gladly remain the reference for property training.

Real Estate for Agencies

Introduction property authorities at Brisbane are dealt with regularly. The central point of this essay is to examine first to what extent Brisbane property agencies face the characteristics of the perfectly competitive business. Secondly, it would analyze the pros and cons of this business about welfare implications using manufacturer and user surplus constructs. The express authority is distinct from the implicit authority in the property. With the explicit authority, the companies accept that the representative would constitute the principal (s). This would normally be in the document but will be an oral statement. The agreement regarding the fee to be given to the representative normally is in the contract. Jocelyn has some experience in the property area today and understands that it is best to take things in work. She receives a request one time from some potential customers that thought her name on the sign before one of her listings. These future customers need to find the family, and Jocelyn invites them to schedule an appointment with her in her job. They get in, and Jocelyn seats down with them. She has already made some work and gets around the work with them. She can present a written statement the customers at the purchase of a new house. These potential customers sign the written statement and they plan showings of the few houses they are involved in. Jocelyn and these customers have formed the express business.

The implicit authority in property comes into existence only by conduct on the role of the agent for the principal (s). There does not get to be a thing in the document, northing specifically held to orally. With the explicit authority in property, there must be an agreement of some sort. The statement may be oral or in the document and specifically says that the representative would present the principal (s). The implicit authority does not say what amount of commission the agent will have for the sale, but the expressed authority will.

The property agent is a special agent who is authorized by the capital to carry through specific specified acts within the class and the setting of the business established by the capital. The real estate employee is the agent of the property agent, irrespective of whether he or she is the employee for purposes of the property force, or the individual contractor of the property agent for national and state income tax reporting purposes. The agent at this actual property transaction oversees his or her employee who acts as the agent of the broker. (Civil Code Â§ 2079.13 (b).) Property agents may work independently or use one or more licensed property agents. In some cases, the property agent may decide to work for another property business as an associate agent. Associate agents have the same qualifications as an individual agent or businessperson, but they are not in charge of the other property brokers they work with. The day-to-day duties of the property agent may differ, but their main role is to function as the go-between for buyers, vendors and their respective brokers.

Real-Estate agents/agencies will identify hundreds or 1000s of attributes for near-zero fees. Custom agent profiles will connect to existing websites and show single-agent lists. Agents will link to this Sysco in block chain from their existing site, or they will set up their site on their website. These terms of giant e-commerce websites like eBay and Amazon have made focused and draconian business practices that benefit from merchants. Large network result, periods of preying upon and absorbing competitors have rewarded them with little to no contest. Pretend you are developing a new system for the local property business. The business needs to make the database of its place listings and need to get access to the citywide multiple listings service used by all property agents. Which design strategy would you suggest for the business of the organization? Reason? Pretend you are producing a new system for the multi-state chain of TV stores. Each shop can get a standard set of TV storage operations

November 1, 2019

(cataloging video product, consumer registration, picture rentals, TV returns, overdue fees, etc.).

Running with people who are informed about the property is important. Property authorities and brokerages are not the only types of corporations that make in the property. There are also business firms and ad authorities. No matter what kind of job the company handles, it is crucial that it engages people who have backgrounds in the property. As a college student, one of the ways of getting the money during vacations is to be as the property agent. The property business involves the purchasing, the marketing, or the rental of lands, buildings or housing services and others. Property business or the real estate agent (Agent) is the person who acts as the intermediary between the sellers and purchasers of property/actual property. They are involved in looking for merchants who trade properties and buyers to purchase attributes. If you are planning on hiring, purchasing or renting property on the land, property Agencies provide a variety of services, whether it is a little quiet house or a vacation rental, Property agents can provide you with the knowledge you want. There is a large variety of rental properties available in San Juan and throughout the land in the beach and hotel fields.

The home today, is a site that can include a complete information of Russian and international property provided by developers; the lower place information provided by property authorities and people; a news bulletin providing you with current and relevant information about real estate; an advertising section; all the relevant online services for making a deal, Together with developer, property business and bank ratings. Whether you are considering purchasing or selling property in Oregon, you are searching for any additional data about, or property at Boardman, you have gone to the good spot. OregonLive.com will help you make Boardman property authorities realtors or agent who can help you buy or sell the house, rent the apartment and get you valuable information about schools in the area, Property industry conditions and more! Property business speaks more languages for the Property business. Therefore, it is better to improve the property business by the Professional property example Retouching Company. They require vivid ways to aggregate the property property business for enriching on colors, ighting, and change and on perspective corrections.

Property hunt, for both purchasing and dealing, it is not as intelligent as in America. There does not appear to be the MLS service here offering the backend information for property sales, and there are a bunch of smaller property offices here making it fragmented industry. Overall, the entire property industry here feels a lot less intelligent than America the way that prepares people to create, acquire, sell, appraise, and manage real property. Includes education in land use process policy, property force, real estate marketing operations, agency administration, business, property examination and assessment, property finance, leased and rental properties, commercial real estate, and property management.

Ray Ito has been used in Can Trust property for nearly two years. Before getting his property license, he was a property manager with a large property business in another neighborhood. Within his early year with Can Trust, he was designated to this residential property league and traded properties totaling $ 3 875 000. He then requested and had the transfer to the trade division. MS. Saunders was a property agent with the local property authority. She had been running in the city, Alabama property industry for almost 24 years. She was acquainted with the subject property because she participated in the assessment of this place and subsequently was the listing agent for the sale. It is the broker price judgment and it is very similar to the assessment. With the broker price opinion with the estimate, you have three families that are sold that are equal to the subject place. With the broker price judgment, you have six houses.

Business relationships in residential property transactions require the legal statement by the property agent (on behalf of the property organization) of the capital, whether the person (s) is a buyer or a seller. The agent and his authorized real estate salespersons (salesmen or agents) then turn into the agents of the capital. The managing agent is a property agent who oversees a group of property brokers or real estate associate agents. Some designated agents also work as the managing agents in their business, while some employ other agents to take the managing agent and take a more hands-off approach to work the agency. Although the license allows them to start their own business as a designated agent and manage other agents as the managing agent, associate agents rather prefer to be under another property broker. This means they have the same roles and duties in the property business that real estate agents do.

The property agent may work independently as a property agent or have different property agents who work for them. Real estate agents must be under the licensed property agent so that only property professionals able to work independently are agents. The real estate business employs one or more property agents. Collective property relates to the actual properties that hold the business activities of an organization that owns or rents and manages property incidental to its main sector, which is not real estate. Corporate property may be contrasted with commercial property, where the job is property. The purpose of commercial property is to make a return and the purpose of Corporate property is to help the enterprise.

Commercial property (CRE) is property used solely for business purposes out to offer the space rather than a living place. Most frequently, commercial property is rented to tenants to perform business. The category of property ranges from one single gas station to a large shopping center. Commercial property includes retailers of all sorts, business areas, hotels, strip malls, restaurants, and convenience shops.

Trade property is a place that is typically rented out for commerce and retail purposes. Investing in trade property requires the acquisition or improvement of attributes that have been designed with the intention of housing commercial tenants. Unlike the residential real estate investor, commercial property investors contract out and take rent from those jobs that occupy a place at their properties, rather than from residential tenants. It should also be noted that natural land bought for the growth of the technical property is also included in the explanation. Continue learning to see more about each one.

One business that gains greatly from economic prosperity is property. As the need for more living space develops with sharp population growth, property authorities can increase property costs. After ConocoPhillips' existence at Darwin, the average cost for the three-bedroom building was $ 660,000. This average for all capital cities in the country was $ 533,000 (Ennis). While that negatively impacts some of the working-class population because of higher competition, long-time residents saw the raise in their new place value. Having won the battle, the property business surprised the national houses with the antic€ "national housing effort at the local level. Across the nation, members of local property authorities and S& Ls mobilized to move local construction agencies, veto construction projects, and refuse housing appropriations or brands. This "national housing rides were more productive in the South and West than in huge eastern and western cities where national housing and urban redevelopment loved governmental assistance (Davies 1966).

The construction industry was the greatest case of separate housing in Michigan. Within the construction business, some social scientists observed that `` property authorities play the largest role in keeping separate societies " (Knowles and Prewitt 26). Property agents created large profits manipulating white concerns of integration and dark desires to flee the ghetto, as demonstrated by the lucrative knowledge of blockbusting. The real estate broker would make the black house to go to an all-white community. After the black house moved in, nervous whites feared, their place values could fail.

The Sudanese female and her boy gave some applications to other property authorities and had telephone calls from them rejecting her request on this ground that she got no quotations from previous real estate agencies and that other applicants did not have to apply to Homes west for bond assistance to rent. It was not feasible for the customer to take references, as she was the recent arrival. (Business entry 16 p.70).

How does business face when it is known edited? Yea that faces with the imperfection. To avoid the problem the Real Estate authorities must receive property business writing Services. There are some services involved in property Photography writing services some of them are generally involved for property agencies exist, Because of the multitude of good feedback for real estate property images online show, increasingly property agencies, corporations, and even homeowners are using the marketing tool. This is until now one of the most effective and efficient ways of dealing and purchasing homes or properties. These requests of these realtors are intense that BEEPEC has rendered its finest companies to respond to these requests.

An occupied property is the art activist program coming out of NYC, running in foreclosures, eviction defense and squatting. They have re-imagined the social concept of the property business by making their own that advertises abandoned properties for jobs, publicizes eviction protection, and promotes instruments and tactics for successful squatting. With one of these most widely respected brands in the whole property business, period 21® will not be matched by other York region, Pa., Property authorities when it comes to knowledge of the local industry and this extensiveness of our lists. Our abundance of education not just benefits customers; it also benefits all property agents who decide to drop their shingle with us. We give all the tools you will want to win.

The responsibility of the property crisis is largely the concern of the lacuna of training of Romanian property authorities. The real estate agent must emphasize the necessity of the fast decrease in costs to fix the situation in the property industry. The industry can continue if we can get the interest zone at 300 euros, concluded the chief economist. The implicit authority in property is the authority that has been formed from the behavior of the principal (or customer) and the agent. It is not the agreement that these two have created in work, but rather, shaped by something that has been made (conduct). Not all states recognize implied authority and rather, be that the agency must have a written statement to be. It may be difficult for the real estate agent to take the fee on sales that lead from implied authorities, as there is no written statement about charges.

As a property agent, there are a couple of other avenues you can make in setting up the business. Working for the property agent business will give you stability, too as the benefit of being surrounded by skilled professionals. However, before you put on to be with the broker office, be confident and ask the following questions: The language surrounding property agents, brokers, and Realtors may be unclear. Real estate agents and property agents are the same cases of licensed property professionals, but they are not the same. To buy or sell property on behalf of others, the person must get appropriate permission from the government governing or licensing structure. The real estate agent's license is the entry-level license that most states need for property professionals.

Expatriates should get plenty of accommodation options regardless of where in France they exist. Most property authorities have place lists displayed in their windows and on their sites. Some property brokers might not be fluent in English, but they would do their best to convey and make appropriate lodging alternatives. Instead, a simple internet search will give lists of free apartments, homes or area stock options. Some French sites give the read English translation. Some bed-and-breakfasts and vacation rentals also provide long-term stays, which are useful while searching for a permanent house.

Real Estate Owned

Property agents are licensed to oversee their businesses. As individual people, agents often sell property owned by others. In addition to helping customers acquire and sell properties, they may help hire or administer properties for the fee. Some run the property office, managing job information and supervising the business of sales agents. In the traditional property transaction, the real estate broker would oversee the work. When selling FSBO houses on your own, the property owner gets to search to see a couple of sites that provide posting houses on the market online. Typically, these types of sites pay a fixed rate, plus the value of important services, such as listing pictures and the field sign. In addition to real estate agents, property agents are essential to the family purchasing process. Agents and Agents do similar business, but property Agents are licensed and able to manage their property jobs. Agents and Agents work together to assist you with the property needs. So, if you want a broker, realtor.com® is the asset.

The commercial property agent's business is much different from that of the residential property agent. Mostly, trading or renting commercial property takes a significantly longer period, and commercial property agents must offer strong analytical data and business information. Agents may be by themselves, for a real estate services business or the trade agent. Most commercial property agents are given on a fee basis. In the reality of property investment, rent to own— a.k.a. The property choice or purchase option— is one of the more investment schemes to get money from real estate. Rent to personal houses is property investment properties, which place investors, lease out to prospective buyers, giving them the chance to get the purchase after the set period (usually 1–3 years).

The choice— also called the property choice or a contract to own provision— gives residential property investors the power to make a deal with the potential customer in which the buyer can rent real estate investments for a set period (typically 1–3 years) before actually buying the residential property. That means owners of residential properties experience the guaranteed monthly income (which is higher than at conventional rentals!). All the previously mentioned investment schemes require the real estate investor to have the income place to make money. Yet, if you are wondering how to do a deal of money at property investing without property control, there are two choices, the first one representing real estate wholesaling. Essentially, the real estate distributor works as an intermediary between property buyers and property sellers in the property transaction. All the property investor must do is to get the vendor, select the finance property to the contract, and deliver the bid to the end-buyer after which he/she walks away with a portion of profits made.

If no one buys the house, the investor turns into the owner and the house is considered the bank owned or REO (property owned) place. Typically, the investor then works with the property agent to put the place on the store. Mostly, REO attributes are sold `` as equals, " which means the investor is trading the house at its new status and can do no repairs or improvements (or give the buyer any credits to fund fix-its). You should rarely, under any circumstance, own the property assets directly in your own family! Most of the time, important property investors have properties through a thing called the limited liability company or LLC. These types of corporations will protect their assets from lawsuits and other risks. Most affluent investors have their family through the LLC as a risk management exercise. As the potential current property investor, it is imperative that you see how LLCs work and why you may need to take them to make the property properties or else real estate investments.

However, like any other kind of finance, entering the reality of property investment comes with several risks. Certainly, each kind of property investment place has its dangers. Nevertheless, successful property investors see that investing in multi-house rentals is less dangerous than investing in different types of finance properties.

The real estate investor having any kind of finance property that is up for rent can face some challenges throughout their property investment business. Having the Airbnb may be a luxurious investment, but this does not give it an easy one. The property investor must consider these challenges and be mindful of how to defeat them before purchasing finance properties to lease them out as Airbnb leases. How to put at the place if you do not get what it takes to accomplish it? Well, some property investors (particularly those having multiple property assets properties or the income place in the area in which they do not go) choose for employing professional property management to take care of their investments. While this is a great thought in some instances, it is not affordable. Therefore, business property management is not recommended for the beginner property investor whose purpose is to create and save money.

Another way of getting money at the property without having to have the income property is by putting the money in REITs. Property finance Trusts are corporations that buy and own multiple investments ranging from flat buildings, through business buildings and shopping malls, to hospitals and huge finance properties. Several people dream of having their own house for their purpose or property purposes. Some investors exist cashing in on students' assistance. These property investments are directly owned property, property limited partnerships, REITs (property finance trusts) and property growth corporations. REIT is the corporation that finances, controls or owns the income-producing property. The investor in such a company owns a liquid interest in the property.

The property investment trust (REIT) is the corporation that owns, and in most cases operates the income-producing property. REITs have numerous cases of technical property, ranging from business and apartment buildings to warehouses, hospitals, shopping malls, hotels, and timberlands. Some REITs employ in financing property. REITs may be publicly traded on better exchanges, public but non-listed, or personal. These two primary cases of REITs are assets REITs and mortgage REITs (REITs). In November 2014, equity REITs were recognized as the different asset classes at the Global business Classification measure by S& P Dow Jones index and MSCI.

Property investment trusts ("REITs") allow people to spend in large-scale, income-producing property. The REIT is a corporation that owns and typically controls income-producing property or similar assets. These may consider business buildings, buying malls, flats, hotels, resorts, self-storage installations, warehouses, and mortgages or loans. Unlike other property companies, the REIT does not produce property attributes to sell them. Rather, the REIT purchases and produces properties mainly to engage them as part of its finance portfolio.

Instead of having property now, investors may also buy shares of the property investment trust (REIT) or shares of the mutual fund that invests in these securities. REITs have and manage the income-producing property. They are regulated by some rules: At least 75 percent of total income must be from rents, benefit from mortgages, or other property investments and, first, REITs must administer at least 90 percent of their assessable income to stockholders every year as dividends.

The REIT is a corporation that owns controls or finances income-producing property. Modeled after mutual funds, REITs allow all investors to have precious property, be the opportunity to make dividend-based income and overall returns, and help communities develop, thrive and revitalize. REITs permit anyone to spend in portfolios of property assets that same way they spend in different industries – through the acquisition of personal company products or the mutual fund or exchange-traded fund (ETF). The REIT is a firm, faith or organization that owns and, in most cases, controls income-producing property and/or actual estate-related assets. Modeled after shared funds, REITs pool the assets of many investors. This allows individual investors to get the share of the income created through trade property ownership, without having to get out and purchase or finance property or possessions. For most people, their biggest "unconventional assets" is property. You may have the property at the 401 (k) through REITs and mutual funds, but you cannot have the deed to the place. You must put up a system if you need to spend the retirement funds in the property place. You also cannot have golden bullion, artwork, or additional collectibles.

REITs, or property investment trusts, permit you to spend in real estate without the personal property. Frequently compared to mutual funds, they are corporations that have a commercial property, e.g., business buildings, retail places, apartments, and hotels. REITs tend to give higher dividends, which gives them a better investment in retirement. Investors who do not want or want that normal income will automatically reinvest those dividends to develop their assets further. If you need a simpler choice to spend in real estate than having property properties or flipping homes, investors should expect property investment trusts or REITs. These trusts put in the property either through primary control of properties or by purchasing mortgages and additional mortgage-related securities. Nevertheless, REITs move in several countries – from marketing to healthcare to residential – so investors are better served trading this sector generally. However, what mix does the most sense? We will investigate this by looking at 10 of the greatest REIT ETF choices to get a day.

One of the most common ways to have property is through the kind of assets called the REIT, which is small for a property investment trust. Property investment trusts do in nearly limitless `` flavors; " for instance, some spend but in commercial property, and others just in apartment complexes. You will sell REITs just as stocks through the business account and those dividends are taxed differently than dividends from funds. Learn how REITs work and whether you should consider having them instead of primary property possession. The REF gives shareholders dividends derived from the profits of a trade, business, residential, or rental property. The most common way to put in property is by investing the money in property investment trust (REIT), which is the corporation that owns and controls income-producing real estate assets. One may also decide to spend now in possession (as opposed to shares of property) through personal REITs, which need significantly higher assets and are generally out of reach for retail investors. For the piece, we are speaking about investing in property as it relates to national REITs.

Refit's also called property finance Trusts represent the corporate investment into property assets owned by REIT stockholders and the income generated by these properties is distributed among shareholders. We all remember property from our next-door neighbor or close friend as a property generating vehicle that would allow us to avoid running this 9-to-5 business. However, what some of us do not realize is that investing in REIT's offering three important benefits that outweigh the direct investment in the slice of place. The REIT (which is said `` REET " and stands for property Investment Trust) is the corporation that gives investments in and owns incoming generating property attributes. Investors get shares of this REIT and the REIT utilizes the money to create investments. This REIT so typically earns income from rent payments or share on property loans.

Property investment trusts (REITs) are the less traditional means to invest in property. What is the REIT? REITs are corporations or trusts that have or pay property investments, and they sell shares to investors who want to get the share of the income given off the property investment. To get money off the home that has increased in value, you must sell the place, which will make time. This is the reason it is important to take three to six months of expenses kept at the emergency fund in addition to the money you put away for upkeep and repairs.

If the place is real estate owned, the funds can then go through the process of attempting to sell this place on its own. It would take to remove some of the liens and additional expenses on the building, and so decide to sell it on the store. Real-estate investors can often take after these properties as banks are not in the business of having hotels and, in some instances, these hotels will be purchased in the discount to its market value. This depreciation cost is not available on REITs (property finance trusts) as you are not investing in property but funds, therefore not offered with the same benefits. Having `` true " property will allow you to get a positive income in the first year and take depreciation to reduce the tax burden to zero. Specific repairs, capital expenditures (conveniences, ceilings, windows, plumbing, etc.), maybe deducted as depreciation reducing the taxation statement on income.

The last tax benefit of purchasing the rental property vs. REIT investment is the 1031 change. Real estate investors who have property properties will defer capital profits when they sell the rental property and have that proceeds to purchase more property assets in the housing industry. REITs do not prepare for the tax reduction. Passive income may be made when owning a rental place if you take over rental property management to a business organization rather than growing into the property owner. There is no arguing that buying the investment place and renting it out through Airbnb is the common way in today's property investment business. In some instances, property investors having the Airbnb short-term rental property have more profits and a higher return on assets than when owning the conventional long-term rental place.

Real Estate License

Property license reciprocity is the arrangement between multiple states providing property agents licensed in one government to be certified in reciprocal states without considering local real estate pre-licensing classes. Reciprocity is state-specific, with some states involving complete re-examination, some involving special testing, and others flatly denying relation to out-of-state licensees. After finishing their real property licensing course to take their real estate agent's permission, and accruing the necessary education needed in their government, Real estate agents then want to get the extra property agent's licensing course, too as give their government's broker's licensing test. This broker's licensing class is typically if the property broker's pre-licensing class and covers similar issues. In New York State, for instance, the agent's licensing class is 45 minutes.

Property agents are required to take property courses and give the property-licensing test for the government or states at which they work, but the real estate license alone does not create the real estate business a broker. The property agent is a business who has kept their training and has passed required tests to get their property agent permission. In cases where people make themselves out to be decent licensed property agents or brokers, the crime of practicing property without permission occurs at each transaction. For instance, if you get one property license in one state, go to another and fail to apply for a property license in this current government, you may not act as a real estate agent. If you decide to do so, each transaction you act in as someone else's agent or representative is considered an individual offense.

The first thing to notice is the difference between the property agent and a broker. The real estate agent is a business that helps people acquire and sell the place. They take the real property permit. One agent also holds the same license and gets that one responsibility; Nevertheless, they are also part of the National Union of Realtors which has the stricter code of ethics when working with consumers and dealing with property sales. Neither an agent nor a realtor is necessarily eligible to be exclusively on investments, which is why it is important to get the investor-friendly true property agent or broker.

When one person first becomes certified to turn into a real estate agent, they receive the property employee's license (some states take the term `` agent ") from the state in which s/he will practice. To get a property permit, the person must get proper work (between 40 and 120 minutes) and pass the state test on property law and practice. To be, salespersons must be associated with (and be under the authority of) the property agent. In Delaware, for instance, this licensing education requires the person to get 99 classroom hours to prepare to go for the state and public exam.

Anyone who wants to be property as an employee, real estate agent, or property agent must first get the license to do so from the government in which they live. State property license requirements differ somewhat from the government to government, but all normally require that the individual complete a minimum amount of property training, apply to the state real estate governing the organization, and give the written test. However, after you have had the government license will you function as a property employee or broker?

In this United States, property agents and salespersons are certified by each state, not by the government. Each government has the real estate "charge" who monitors and licenses property agents and agents. For instance, some states simply permit attorneys to make software to move real property. Where different states give the licensed property agent. Government forces are specifying the types of relationships that may be between customers and real estate licensees, and the legal obligations of real estate licensees to present customers and members of the public. Property brokers and agents must be certified everywhere in the U.S. They typically gain the permit after passing state-administered property tests. Some states need only the standard property license, while others need a technical property license. Future trade property agents will get state-specific requirements by contacting the government's property commission or department of property.

Real estate agents are licensed to help merchants sell and buyers purchase property and are mostly licensed to control negotiate and organize sales under the supervision of the property agent. Discuss and arrange may think to show the property, listing the property, filling in contracts, naming arrangements, and purchase contracts. Real estate agent: Anyone who earns a property license will be named a property agent, whether the license is as a sales business or an associate agent. They see lists on the double listing service and help you buy or sell the home. Government requirements differ, but in all states, you must take the minimum number of courses and pass the test to get permission.

The passing course on the state property-licensing test does not quite think you have a license, however. The property employee (representative) is licensed to be on behalf of the agent and may not function as a property agent independently. Consider getting the property agent early in the licensing process. Once you have finished the relicensing training requirements and passed the test, you and the agent will both want to fill final work with the government. Once the structure is accepted, the license will be released, and you may learn property under the support of the agent.

Before we get into our pros and cons database, we must suggest that there is no such thing as the technical property license —any individual with the up-to-date property license can sell commercial properties. This is the good thing about getting a property license: You have the flexibility to deliver some different types of properties! Not everyone who takes the real estate permit in Florida turns into the REALTOR and dedicates to the transaction-based transactions. Some people have the property license to help increase the odds of landing on the ideal investment place (Chen, 2019). Others can have this permission to more effectively run the property management business.

Some property investors ask whether it is worth the time and money to take the property license. There are some advantages of having the permit for property assets. Using the own property permission to make better deals, networking with authorized brokers, and getting more money with commissions are all incentives for getting the extra time and cost to get a real estate license. These required 30-hour Texas pre-license classes give up the 180 minutes needed for the Texas property permit and lay a strong foundation for the property business. The rules of property 1, Principles of property 2, philosophy of business, philosophy of Contracts, property management and Promulgated Contract Forms courses cover government police, ownership, valuation and brokerages, as well as real-world discussions about mortgages, Lending forces, and other consumer-based ideas. The Texas property committee approves these classes. Class right for the early class expires six months from acquisition. Extension choices are free.

Government laws govern property laws, agent responsibilities, and licensing and therefore any data here may and probably would vary by government. In addition, it is commonly necessary for property managers to be certified in property, too. Most property brokers are employed in residential property listing and sales. Different companies seek out candidates with vocational real estate education or a property license. Work in real estate growth, property administration, real estate business, urban planning, affordable housing management, property management, and construction for the elderly are particularly sought after. If getting back to education INS' 'tone alternative, you will always invest in online classes to increase your knowledge and develop your skills. Likewise, do not underestimate the amount of on-the-job education.

You may want to go off in the entry-level job, but when you see this job, you will make up the ranks.

Different companies seek out candidates with vocational real estate education or a property license. Work in real estate growth, property administration, real estate business, urban planning, affordable housing management, property management, and construction for the elderly are particularly sought after (Chen, 2019). If getting back to education is' 'tone alternative, you will always invest in online classes to increase your knowledge and develop your skills. Likewise, do not underestimate the amount of on-the-job education. You may want to go off in the entry-level job, but when you see this job, you will make up the ranks.

No matter where you go, you will have to take a pre-licensing class from the accredited property licensing school before you will go for the property license test. The required amount of time varies by the government. In California, for instance, applicants must take three property courses totaling 135 minutes. In New York, this way takes 75 minutes. Every government has several rules and ordinances for property agent licensing. Most taxes require a certain number of classes to get the property permission before you will get the licensing test. In Colorado, you must get 160 minutes of training; different states represent more and some much less. Some states are still thinking about making it necessary that all property agents have at least a bachelor's degree to take the property license. I authored the article that goes into the information on how difficult it is to take the permit here.

The easy answer is, "it depends." it largely depends on where the individual needs to learn property. Growing into a real estate agent requires a government license. Each state regulates its own property licensing operation, and each government's rules or rules are somewhat different. However, there are a couple of fundamental requirements that are usually consistent. Anyone who needs to function as a property agent or agent must first be licensed to do so by the government licensing structure. While you do not have to be the licensed property broker if you are purchasing possession for yourself or trading property you have, you do have to have the permit to purchase or sell the property for others for the fee or profit. Therefore, for somebody to function as a property agent for someone else, the person must get a property license.

The property agent, in contrast, is someone who holds a more advanced property permit. Like the agent, a property agent will purchase and sell property on behalf of customers but may do so independently and without running under the supervision of another property broker. Agents may also use other property agents to work for them, or make a property business, while those who simply have the property agent's permit cannot.

The active property sales representative license is the next step. This allows the holder to study property under the direction (sponsorship) of the person who holds the property agent's permission (Chen, 2019). During the term, the sales representative may not receive any compensation for the property transaction nor get the property fee except through the sponsoring agent.(b) He or she is a certified property agent, certified real estate broker-salesperson or certified property employee, whether his or her license is involved or inactive. The disclosure may be achieved concerning himself or herself as an agent, licensee, employee, agent or broker-salesperson, whichever is suitable.

It is illegal for any authorized property agent to use or settle, directly or indirectly, any individual for performing any of the acts for which the license is needed who is not a licensed real estate broker, Or a property employee licensed under the agent using or compensating him or her; allowed, However, that a licensed property agent may give the fee to the broker of another state. No real estate employee shall be used by or receive compensation from any person except the agent under whom he is in this moment licensed. (Commerce and Professions Code § 10137). There is some significance, although. Property agents may work as agents, but agents cannot be as agents, at least not without the broker's permission. Agents who say property advice must also get a property license. What are those great distinctions between these titles and what represent these similarities? See on to get out. The property agent is one-step over the property agent. The broker generally has more training and subject-matter training than the agent does, but not forever. The property agent may work independently or employ real estate salespersons to get under them.

The property agent has kept his or her training past the real estate-agent point and has passed the state property agent license test. Property agents may be as separate brokers or have different agents working for them: Brokers who have passed the broker test, but who prefer to be under another broker is typically called a real estate associate broker. The associate agent may share in the business profits above and beyond the regular agent fee. Each government has a different structure for licensing real estate agents and property agents. In most states, there are real estate salesperson and property agents. A property salesperson must be under the property agent to take an active licensee. To turn into a broker, most states require a certain amount of time as the employee, too as more training and experimentation. Some states have other names for agents and salespeople, e.g., Co, which calls beginning agents broker associates and has employing agents or individual agents.

The real estate agent is a master in the business who has taken and passed all required property courses, along with the property licensing test at the government at which he or she intends to work (Chen, 2019). As this starting point for most of those moving into this property area, it is the most comprehensive of these titles. Brokers are also referred to as property fellows. The real estate agent is a master who has passed that required property courses and licensing tests in the state where he intends to be. That is the starting point for most property professionals, and the agent name is the most encompassing. An agent is the property broker who is a part of the human Association of Realtors. Realtors must endure by this union's criteria and code of ethics. In addition, the real estate agent has continued his training and received the broker's permission. Agents can work independently or use different agents. The property associate agent is an agent that is working on the broker's permission.

Like property sales agents, their government must certify agents. To qualify for the broker license, one must first take a reasonable property sales representative license and business under the license for several years. In some states, agents must have two years of experience working as the sales representative, but some states need just one year of education. Different states maybe three. Property license reciprocity symbolizes the ability of the agent to be certified in a new government from their existing home state permission. Property portability allows out-of-state agents to perform transactions within states, using local laws. To improve, we compiled permit relation and portability principles for all 50 states.

The 28-hour online course, from significant knowledge from Florida property Principles, Practices& philosophy, is meant for property sales associates and agents who currently take involuntary inactive Florida real estate licenses. The way satisfies the education requirements required to reactivate the license, including the required two tests. Training activities offer the interactive method of thought reinforcement and self-testing. Pictures give education on concepts that are difficult to understand. Each state requires that you complete the state-administered real estate licensing test before having the property license. The test frequently includes a public component and the state-specific component.

Both parts of this investigation are designed to test the knowledge of property practices, policies, and language to ensure all authorized professionals follow the sector on the equal platform of basic industry knowledge. Some schools offer real estate exams, training classes. The government does not take these test preparation courses. This licensing test is a choice for TREC to confirm you know the material before they give you the real estate license and allow you to present buyers and sellers in real estate transactions. This experiment must be difficult enough to confirm that you have the knowledge required to be a skilled property professional. This licensing test is so difficult that only around 59 percent of students go on any given exam time. The good news is that selecting a top-tier property education will dramatically change the chances of reaching the test. For Ace able Agent students, this passing rate jumps to 92 percent!

Real Estate Websites

Need to know if the site is being SPAMMED? Backlink watcher is a great monitor method that outlines all the connections and sites that are heading to the property site. It is a great exercise to health check the property site every month. First signs of e-mail attacks make you ready and fix this problem as soon as possible. Speaking of property sites, Mash visor is THE site to apply if you are trying to make THE investment place through property analysis. Mash visor allows you to see thousands of lists at various states, cities, and localities across the US and cuts the 3-month property search into 15 hours. If for instance, you are considering Boston property, all you want to do is identify this community (or metropolis) list into our web search engine and the part is taken care of by the site. Mash visor's finance property computer can show you measures for Coca return, cap and residence rates, and estimated property (Chen, 2019).

Course, another of the must-have real estate investment resources is property sites. Even though mobile apps continue moving up in popularity, websites remain a reliable source of common property knowledge, too as of information on attributes. You can utilize sites as the property-investing asset in so many ways: The Ethereal-based block chain property offering and acceptance platform integral with any property site. This structure also provides online renting services and the property agreement form contractor customizable for any nation or government. Shelter Zoom offers a method in a business that aims to better safety and clarity in what traditionally has been a broken and opaque process.

Property sites are all about shown and you just take a couple of minutes to convey the brand. The property site for the Cunningham Team, made using the true Geeks platform, is elegant and actionable. Using the complex style building as the background to the search menu brings depth and a sense of what the coming house might look like. The search choice is complemented by this ability to get search outcomes with friends and family via e-mail, Facebook, and Twitter. There is an increase in the usage of web pages in the property business industry. In January 1995, about 100 property sites provided properties on the market. By the end of 1996, this number had grown up to about 8,000 sites. Some of these websites affected the house pages of single properties while others included lists of around 500,000 properties. While full selling and buying data was initially lacking in the number of these websites, this is quickly growing into the number of the listings. In 1999, about 9 percent of all web pages on the net are related with actual estate.52

According to CRE Online, the large property investment site established in 1995, the best strategy for buying the investment property level and selling it up is to design the property investments from the property industry cycle. This implies that you should be purchasing the investment place at the side of the cycle when prices are reduced. So, once you have decided it is time to move with the income place, you should move till the level (between these past stable and earlier downturn periods), when prices are high. It sounds like a wise decision, no. These real-estate trades that seem the prettiest and are easiest to find—such as purchasing a place that has a resident and organization in place, joining the crowdfunding site, or purchasing into a publicly-traded real estate investment trust—yield the lowest returns. The most rewarding opportunities are those people no one else knows about, which you see and make.

It is no secret these times that you MUST have the site for property commerce. Good property site can the necessary things to improve consumer access to the product quickly. Particularly, with property business, agent sites help provide local searches that allow homebuyers to easily seek out agents.

If you would also want to search for commercial property properties yourself, you may see commercial property listings on such sites as the trade property Listing delivery or LoopNet. Still, if you decide to see for yourself, you will have to perform the following without the assistance of the experienced agent: The whole service contract is the most common type of commercial lease for office buildings. With the whole service contract, the rent is all-inclusive. Before performing the contract, departments must apply an off-campus contract approval form to the Associate VP, property. Real estate property approval forms can be downloaded from the estate, construction property site. After acceptance of the contract transaction and implementation of the contract, departments must ask the Purchase Order or BU amount from Procurement for the total contracted payment payments at the period of the lease, to ensure appropriate recording of these dealings and to change payments.

ForSaleByOwner.com is on the mission to empower merchants and buyers with all the resources they want to deliver or purchase properties immediately (ForSaleByOwner.com, 2019). With a suite of easy-to-use marketing tools that promote listings across the network of high property sites and the product database Service, how-to guides and live consumer support, we've represented the running "by owner" property site in the USA since 1999. More than ever the property site is recognized by agents and brokers as a valuable tool to create leads and interact with customers. For over 20 years IDXCentral.com has been specializing in property site innovation, IDX sales, and consolidation (IDXCentral.com, 2019). We would like to show you what we will do. Learn more about our property site services or meet us today.

Darren is an entrepreneur, product director, and property innovator. Long before Zillow and Trulia, Darren co-founded SeattleRentals.com in the past 2002, one of those first property sites in this nation. He has gone on some of the most important tech productions of our period that have reached a large scale and influence in corporations like Microsoft, Amazon, Expedia, AOL and more. The following year, for an undisclosed amount estimated to be as up as $ 200 million, Warner purchased the five-parcel getaway compound at Montecito, the palatial land dominated by an Italianate mansion. (One California real-estate site says that place is currently valued in $ 160 million.) He proceeded to hold out his portfolio through some of the first to mid-2000s, bringing the near Montecito land Association, the San Sedro farm and the 4 Seasons go hotel in Santa Barbara, among other high-profile properties.

As this name indicates, Auction.com is a site that focuses on construction auctions. They sell all types of property including foreclosures, roe's, small sales, notes, trade real estate, luxury property, new business, and estate. These auctions happen online, locally on-site or at courthouses, too as at living mega-auctions at meeting halls. Canaveral: Auctioning properties is a recent process in the luxury property world. As a luxury property agent, our CEO knows what the person is searching for. These new companies that auction luxury properties are fortunate, but none exist on the block chain, and none allow transactions to happen at cryptocurrencies. We are this beginning. It looks like every few months an issue or the property site anoints the new community (s) as the "hottest new community" in NYC (including, um, us), and this week is no different. Property Shark has anticipated that East New York could take the most happening community that the coming year that New York Post first reported.

In publication time the place's job on property site Red fin stated `` accepting back up offers. " The listed cost for the mixed construction and retail area at the Exposition arena is $ 1,900,000. This list is described as `` placed at the heart of the Make Jefferson Beautiful Street work. This offer presents a unique growth opportunity near to USC as the exit strategy. "

Each government's property licensing requirements are distinct. The government's property commission site can identify the official relicensing requirements. Kaplan Real Estate training provides two pages that narrow the knowledge gap down (kapre.com, 2019). The ways to Licensing page is planned to appear, in simple ways, what it takes to grow authorized in each state. Additionally, Kaplan provides a page devoted to each state's property licensing and continuing training requirements. Find this link below for the state's pages. The teacher should tell how to plan, spend and spend on the licensing test (if not, see the state's property committee website). Tests are computerized and consist of two components – a national component on common property rules and practices and the state-specific area that covers the government's property forces. Each segment is scored individually, and you must get a passing degree on both parts to go. If you go one or both parts, you will have the chance to take the test.

If this target people are those looking to purchase place, what is the actual journey they are on? Mainly, the property is initially sourced via property sites, display house lands, or more recently, apartment off-the-plan ads. If that is the prevailing method of communicating alternatives to the world, it sounds reasonable that property flipping is general. Housing is treated as the product you get, full and prepared, for the value. Moreover, the existence of property brokers and the Internet, e.g., auctions sites and property agent sites help facilitate the process of selling these properties today. It has made the property assets more simple, accessible and positive. In the way, there is an amount of interest in property assets so far lifting the number of properties (JAMES CHEN, 2019).

Any asset that is not property is regarded as a portable place. To further complicate definitions, movable possession is private possession. Immovable property is property, including a mansion, barn, shed, water, porch and any property that will not be picked up and went. Where these definitions turn into significant is the tax period. Property gives property tax. The private place is taxed differently. For beginner property investors, it is a great idea to see exactly what the place tax is. The property tax is a tax that is made for the property place. It is from the amount of the investment property and changes from government to government. As a summary, the amount for the property tax is seen by multiplying the property tax rate by the amount of the investment placed in the property industry.

Well, no, there exist no states with no place taxation. The phrase is even used throughout the property-investing world because there are many states that have such a tiny property tax charge that it is essentially minimal. This return on assets and positive income are untouched by the property tax on the investment place in such states. Today more than ever, it is crucial for real estate investors to analyze property taxation and attempt to make states with no place tax. That is all because of one facet of this 2018 tax campaign: This top on SALT property tax deductions. While SALT property tax deductions even use under this 2018 tax campaign, they have been capped in $ 10,000. For property investors who have the investment place in states with higher property tax, the results at them giving higher taxes overall.

Withal rating number two among these states with no property tax, Birmingham property is seeing greater than ever for beginner property investors are. Not only can property investors gain from almost no property tax and a higher return on investment, but also other components give Birmingham property places on the market a good choice. Another reason why the property finance appeals to some investors the tax benefits and deductions is provided but to property investors. For instance, the income generated from the investment place is tax-free. Additionally, property investors can calculate nearly all expenses associated with having an investment property, e.g., property taxes, mortgage interests, insurance, and operation expenses. Just how much the property investor will calculate depends on his/her property income.

The last reason why the property assets are more lucrative is the tax benefits and deductions provided only to property investors. One example of tax benefits is that the income that the finance place generates is tax-free. Additionally, when property investors get to deliver investment properties and reinvest these profits, they cannot give capital gains tax. Another important benefit of putting in residential attributes is that the residential property investor is entitled to tax breaks for property reduction, property protection, repair repairs, travel expenses, legal fees, and investment property taxes. This administration also provides lower taxation rates for those investing in long-term property investments. These property tax rewards are a huge incentive for some property investors to get residential properties (JAMES CHEN, 2019).

Property investors also have the power to determine if they need to spend in trade Property or residential real estate. When investing in the latter, there are some other types of residential finance attributes to put in, e.g., single-family houses, multi-family houses, condominiums, townhomes, etc. Another option is to invest in conventional property or Airbnb finance properties.

Comparing to other investments like trade property or the stock exchange, residential properties are good property investments and, if done correctly, most risk-free! For property investors who are not also keen on taking risks and seek to ensure the higher rate of returns on the investment, residential property investment does the most sense. As a summary, property investing in the property industry has fewer risks than product assets, particularly when investing in property for the long term. The longer property investors give investment properties, the fewer risks of failure they have because home costs and assets develop with experience. Additionally, the property investment can usually have value since property properties are tangible assets, unlike the product investment, which might fall in value any time. Moreover, the more investment properties the property investor buys and owns the lesser associated risks he/she encounters.

In property investment, there are several property finance property types to choose from. When property investors decide to buy a condominium, a townhouse, or a similar kind of property investment place in the planned neighborhood, they should be informed that they are obliged to join the group's homeowner's union (HOA) and give monthly or yearly HOAs fees. So, what is the homeowner's union and what does the property investor get to learn before joining one? Property investors looking for finance properties are expected to go across at least a couple of attributes that are part of homeowners' associations (HOA). Some property investors wince when they see `` homeowners union " because living within these HOA limits often means more business and monthly fees. Nevertheless, HOAs are not almost as bad as they are frequently depicted, and there are mostly as many advantaged as disadvantages.

Homeowners associations often have limitations on hiring, too. For instance, a property investor looking to rent out or sell property properties might want to take the HOA card's approval on the current prospective tenant. Some homeowners' associations simply provide renting 15 percent of the property properties within the neighborhood, while proprietors must occupy the remainder. These limitations make it difficult for property investors owning investment properties to get the profit on the investment place within the HOA (JAMES CHEN, 2019).

Real Estate Investments

Real estate investment is the best choice to spend money. Point. Whether its $ 10,000 or $ 100,000, through realty investment or passive property investment, there are so many benefits to growing into a property investor. Here are three reasons that get property the best choice to spend $ 10,000: As the minor investor, you want something that offers a better return on investment with very little risk. While there is some danger to traditional property investment, it is just not as dangerous as other types of currency assets. Look at the property industry. Some enter the world of property investment, but not everyone turns into a successful property investor. Why then? Well, while giving money in property is the best way to create property, real estate investment is not as easy as purchasing the rental place and looking for it to start generating profits. Productive property investors not just spend their wealth, but also their time and energy when it comes to property investment. Moreover, certain important success factors need to be considered before purchasing the investment property and starting the investment business (JAMES CHEN, 2019).

As a summary, property finance has fewer risks than product investment, particularly when investing in property for the long term. First, since property investment properties are tangible assets, they can always have value. Funds, in contrast, are intangible assets and will put all their worth any time. In the property investing industry, more than half of these assets properties are single-family houses. Some property investors prefer them at different types of property finance properties because of their lower purchase cost, lower property taxes, lower maintenance costs, higher profit, higher appreciation, and many more benefits.

At property investment, the income of finance attributes is the sum of income that the property investor earns after paying off all expenses, taxes, and mortgage payments. The future danger associated with property investment is the prospect of generating a negative income instead of a positive one. This implies that expenses, taxes, and mortgage payments are completely higher than that property income, which results in missing wealth. Purchasing the investment place does not automatically ensure 100 percent occupancy and immediate profits. In real estate investment, there is the possibility of high vacancy, which is a great danger to property investors' rental income, as it will generate bad income. Furthermore, since renters are the source of property income at real estate investment, vacancy is the large danger for property investors who rely on property income to give off their mortgage, insurance, property taxes, and other expenses.

As previously mentioned, there are some investment strategies and ways to tell this question of how to do a deal of money in property investment. Thus far, we have talked about how to get money from residential property finance properties. Nevertheless, these are not the only things for place investors to take! Investing in trade property means that real estate investor rents out the investment place to businesses (nonresidents). Since jobs generally produce more income than people do, commercial property investment properties generate higher income and return on investment.

It starts without saying that the primary reason why people follow the property investment job is to get money from finance attributes— which is why property investors are constantly searching for the most profitable investments in real estate. In real estate investment, property investors get money from positive income and understanding— both can be talked about as features of most lucrative investments in property. Before going into tips on how to get any rental property into a positively geared investment place, property investors should learn how to select better property investments. Better property investments would be much easier to get into a positively geared investment place. Focus on these matters when selecting the rental place:

The rental place calculator— a.k.a. The finance place computer— is the online property investing way in which property investors input some essential information about the real estate investment property (such as the purchase price, the funding method, the currency finance, etc.). This way then provides them with all the important numbers needed to determine whether to take for the income place. Since the income property is rooted in its property industry, the prosperity of the income place relies on the prosperity of the industry. To get the best place to purchase an investment property for a successful and lucrative property investment business, the property investor must search for specific elements at the position or a real estate market. Keep learning to see the three major elements that place investors should search for to get the best place to purchase an investment property in the US housing industry (JAMES CHEN, 2019).

Mash visor provides property investors with the best property investment tools to do a complete property industry analysis, e.g., mash visor's finance property calculator and the heat map. Within hours, a property investor will easily find the best place to purchase finance property and examine various investment properties across the US housing industry from other measures including rental income, cash on cash return, cap rate, And furtherer! Go here to begin examining investment properties and to get the best place to purchase finance property in the US housing industry with Mash visor!

Disposable income from property investment may be the world. Firstly, take the time to make better property investments. So, focus on increasing property income and diminishing finance property expenses. These will be made for any rental place, making it into the positively geared place sooner rather than later. The second reason why residential property finance is the greatest investment strategy to make money is that residential finance attributes are simple to pay. Funding is the fear for some property investors; however, it is not as bad as some might imagine. The property industry is large, and the property investor would come to know that there are many alternatives for investment property finance. The greatest financing choices for residential property finance are mortgage loans, bad moneylenders, and personal moneylenders.

Having the mortgage is the most common investment property finance choice for property investors— it is a bank loan particularly for property investment. Property investors go to a bank (or the mortgage agent) and apply for the debt, which requires them to move the down payment. Generally, most lenders need a limit of 20 percent of the income property's purchase cost as out payment. For instance, to pay the $ 100,000 income property, a property investor would just have to lay down $ 20,000 in payment, and this mortgage would protect the remaining $ 80,000. Investing is the tool that the property investor can have to create a portfolio of assets attributes. Having the mortgage for purchasing real estate property finance makes property investors leverage to invest in more investment properties with less money down! Let us take one example for a more statement: Most mortgage loans involve this property investor to move out 20 percent of the property's purchase cost as out payment, while the bank (or mortgage broker) finances the other 80 %. Let us say you move 20 percent down for the acquisition of the $ 100,000 property assets (JAMES CHEN, 2019).

However, property investors have several choices to make property investing with less money down by getting the loan. Traditional mortgage loans are the most common in this property investment sector for beginner property investors. Other funding methods are difficult currency loans, personal currency loans, and owner funding. Focus on realizing what is needed of you to get these loans and how much you want to get. When following the kind of property investment strategies, you will need a reliable source of finance, e.g., the traditional loan (mortgage), private payment, or funds contributed by a real estate partner. Furthermore, not all purchase and make investment properties are the ones— they range from single-family houses, through multi-family houses, to whole apartment buildings. Property investors want to learn how to measure deals, which involves a complete comparative property industry analysis in addition to the investment property analysis.

The first part determines the position at which you are planning on investing. Positioning is a significant element in determining property assets' success and profit. Briefly, to get lucrative property assets, property investors must purchase investment properties at higher demand locations. Why is not measuring the position of the investment property a misconception? There is one general misconception that the only way to spend in property is through purchasing an investment property and leasing it out to get money. The assumption is understandable; however, in the large world of property investment, some investment strategies do not require primary property ownership or purchasing investment property!

Even as there are many investment property types, there are also several investment schemes! As the property investor, the initial investing strategy you take to get on is whether you need to remain part of the property investing industry for the long term or the short term. Both investment strategies have proven to be successful in attaining business freedom, and each comes into several proper investment strategies. The real estate investor has the power to achieve stable income, profit from property appreciation, and take a different property investment portfolio all without the hassle of purchasing an investment property and the current obligations of being the landowner! In the section, we talk about four other investment strategies for you to invest in a property that does not require immediate property ownership or purchasing an investment property (JAMES CHEN, 2019).

First, up we get real estate monies and property finance trusts (REITs). In the risk of oversimplifying, these finance vehicles— as their name indicates —put in the property. It may put directly into this property and make income from rent or via mortgage loans at which income is generated from benefit payments. These represent a significant part of alternative investments— I mostly find 40–50 percent + of alternative investment portfolios comprising of REITs. The forward investment scheme to get money without property ownership is investing in property finance trusts. REITs are the greatest when taking how to do a deal of money at real estate passively. With the investment scheme, the property investor buys shares of the REIT that invests in multiple investment projects. Forget about the trouble of turning into the property owner, dealing with renters, and collecting rent! Investing in REITs allows the property investor not only with passive income but also with the diversified finance portfolio!

When investment for the longer term, the most common investment strategy is the buy-and-hold. Different investment strategies include rent-to-own, rent-to-rent, investing in property investment trusts (REITs), and even trade property investment. Some think that investment in REITs is the best and easiest way to get passive income and achieve financial freedom through property investment. As for short-term investment schemes, they allow fix-and-flips, wholesaling, and Airbnb leases. The huge positive of the set business in multifamily property investing beyond simply generating passive income is a limited liability. Property investors who are a passive investment in multifamily households that go south in the property industry are just responsible for no more than the sum of these assets through the limited partnership.

If you are an authorized capitalist, you will invest in property crowdfunding. Property crowdfunding is the middle ground of active and inactive property assets. It is dynamic in the meaning that these investors decide on the place they put in, rather than having the corporation dictate that place. Besides this, it is passive in some respects. For example, the investor may spend smaller quantities, say, $ 5,000, and even higher returns. Likewise, this capitalist is not in charge of administration and rent collection. Crowdfunding offers a good and productive choice on how to get money in real estate passively. When learning how to spend $ 10,000 in property, you will discover that most choices do not revolve in conventional, immediate property investment. Rather, you turn into a passive investor, relying on professionals in the property investment sector to do that work for you. This makes the real estate assets even more stable and reliable, with a small probability (JAMES CHEN, 2019).

The reality of property investment consists of several property investment schemes and ways to make money the income property investor. Do not let that drown you! Property experts have held that specific investment schemes guarantee to make money at the property for the long term, short term, and even without having to have the rental property! Property investment has never been that simple before as with the mash visor's rental property computer! As a property investor, one of the businesses to succeed in the investment job is to value the investment property before purchasing it to ensure that it can be profitable. The beginner property investor might ask: How can property investors still do this? Well, they want the real estate investing tool that provides them with the numbers and calculations needed to assess the property investment place. Here is where the rental place computer gets in handy!

Mash visor's investment property calculator allows property investors to calculate the cap rate, payment on payment return, and positive income of the finance place before purchasing it. Additionally, the real estate investment tool offers property investors with readily estimated and precise outcomes considering these measures for 1000s of investing attributes across the US housing industry to analyze between other investment properties and identify the most profitable investments in real estate to make the best investing decisions (JAMES CHEN, 2019)!

Mash visor is the online platform that allows property investors with real estate finance information analysis to enable them about how to spend on a property and give money. When you go up for Mash visor, you will take hold of the best property investment tools to make and study finance attributes in any government, city, and community across the US housing market! To begin searching for and examining the greatest investment properties in the city and community of choice, click here. Mash visor is the online platform accessible to both skilled and novice property investors. It provides information analysis to enable them to make wise property investment decisions. Mash visor also provides the number of property investment tools for getting started at property finance, including the investment property computer, property finder, the Mash meter, and the Heat map. Additionally, mash visor's Knowledge center includes 1000s of blogs and guides that cover all facets of property investing in the US construction industry. To discover more about our result, go here.

Mash visor provides current and emerging property investors with the best investment tools to successfully perform a complete property industry analysis, e.g., mash visor's finance property calculator, the real estate investing tool that allows the property investor to make and examine various investment properties across the region from other measures. Property investing for beginners is both an interesting and intimidating endeavor. Many people are drawn to the property investing industry for that more rewards it promises them in these long and short terms. Nevertheless, not every property investor joins this class of productive property investors. Reason? Well, there are specific elements that define the success of the assets, and it is up to the property investor to confirm to understand them.

Property investment is not that different from other types of finance. All the property investor must do is to determine the best spots to spend in property to ensure a productive and profitable investment. Property markets with these components mentioned above are considered the best places to invest in property because they represent the highest possible with the least amount of danger. Property investors should consider these factors to narrow down their options and make the best property industry, and then choose the investment place within the industry. For the same reason, before committing to the real estate assets, Property investors must do the property industry investigation in addition to the investment property investigation to get the best profitable investment properties with a higher return on investment. One of the most used measures that the property investor should always keep in mind to determine that profit and return on assets is the payment on payment move (JAMES CHEN, 2019).

One mistake that beginner property investors get when having started in property finance is not performing the real estate industry analysis! The property industry analysis is the process of assessing investment properties to investigate anticipated income and risks. That can decide whether having started in property investment is a great outcome. The property industry is the large figure; there are dozens— if not hundreds— of other property investment schemes, niches, and themes to make money as a property investor. Property investment involves the ability to decrease risk and attention to detail, neither of which are the consequence of bad thinking. To blindly follow the property investing business is to learn ignorance, as the world of the property investing industry is always changing and uncertain. Those who are not made for this fast-paced situation are ready to change their careers as property investors.

Commercial Real Estate

Some businesses have the buildings they inhabit. However, the more normal scenario is that the place is leased. Normally, the investor owns the business and collects rent from each sector that controls there. Commercial property rates—the cost to occupy the place at the stated period—is customarily quoted in annual rental dollars per square meter. Conversely, residential property rates refer to an annual amount or the monthly rent. The first and most common way to increase rental income or positive income from trade property attributes for rent is by optimizing the usage of this location within the technical property. If you have purchased the trade property for rent that is yet not fully finalized, consider ending these incomplete components by separating the surface in a sense that provides as many offices as possible and reasonable.

Another good example of extra services that increase rental income or positive income of trade property properties is room or storage area. There are some possible ways for property investors to use the area to make additional property income. One way is to simply rent out authorities without parking area and pay the additional fee for parking at the property (jointly with the monthly lease), or to lease the parking lot on an hourly or daily basis. Another way is to offer a free room for everyone and provide the covered place for the fee. Some commercial property investors believe encouraging rental income or positive income by reducing the quantity of care. While the way may be at sometimes, it is more likely to react. Commercial property attributes collect a lot more wear and tear than residential property attributes. Thus, normal maintenance is more possible than to be stuck with emergency replacement costs or costly fixes.

A practical example of smart contracts and items exist in the arena of trade property. Block square proposes to take the `` Ethereal of trade property ''. Attributes can be tokenized. Among these benefits, this would give a commercial property more liquid assets and with the possibility for more people to enjoy the advantages. The beginning as the commercial investor is realizing that trade property is valued differently from residential properties. Unlike residential property, the income from commercial property is typically associated with the functional square film. Additionally, technical property rentals typically last longer than those of residential rentals do. These two factors help illustrate why the commercial property investor has the greater potential to get a higher income (JAMES CHEN, 2019).

Have you ever thought about shifting from residential to trade property investment? Although residential and commercial attributes both have proven to be superior and lucrative investments, trade property investment might be a better choice for property investors who are ready to attempt a large venture. Commercial property is any place except for a single-family house or a residential lot in the community. The technical property industry is handled very similarly business and residential property markets. The trade property industry goes through difficulties but like any other investment industry investments into the commercial property will be a very smart decision.

Commercial property is any place except for a single-family house or a residential lot in the community. The technical property industry is handled very similarly business and residential property markets. The trade property industry goes through difficulties but like any other investment industry investments into the commercial property will be a very smart decision. Trade property business and residential real estate business are the main categories from which to decide. Commercial property business normally requires funding for multi-family houses, purchasing centers, industrial and business properties. Residential property business, in contrast, requires funding for private/individual houses (JAMES CHEN, 2019).

The commercial property loan or commercial hard currency debt is a mortgage debt secured by the lien on trade, rather than a residential, place. Trade property (CRE) refers to any income-producing property that is used exclusively for business purposes, e.g., retail malls, business complexes, hotels, and flats. Finance, including the acquisition, growth, and operation of these properties, is typically achieved through commercial property loans. Much like the residential property broker, the commercial property broker represents merchants, purchasers, property owners or lessees of trade property. Yet, since trade property transactions tend to be more difficult than residential transactions, trade property agents generally have more business experience and training than their residential counterparts do.

The earlier field of focus for Drone Base in on the property and property-related enterprise sections, including commercial property, residential real estate, property business and growth, real property insurance and the like. I do not doubt that nearly every part of the property built, inventoried, supervised, rented, Sold or surveyed (whether residential or commercial) in the next few years would get the air picture taken via drone as the core portion of its biography or dossier. The primary sections of the property sector are residential real estate, trade property, and business real estate. The residential aspect concentrates on the purchasing and selling of properties used as houses or for non-professional uses. The commercial sector consists of property used for business purposes; common cases include marketing and business location. Business property is comprised of attributes used for manufacture and industry: Factories, plants, etc.

As we mentioned above, all technical properties are zoned for one specific purpose. The store is a good example of the commercial property place zoned for business purposes. Different commercial property zoning includes business, marketing, restaurant, and leisure. This kind of zoning commands the sort of job that will be out of the technical business. Commercial property force is the class of property law that establishes standards for trade rentals and the purchase and sale of commercial property. Commercial property attorneys who are familiar with commercial contract policies will help you examine possible rental contracts and prevent future pitfalls. The property lawyer will also help inform you of whether hiring or purchasing a trading place would be best for the job. Additionally, the property lawyer will inform you of whether the proposed business would comply with local land use and zoning laws where the trade place could be (JAMES CHEN, 2019).

Purchasing commercial property would typically take more direct costs when compared to leasing commercial property. This is because businesses normally have trade property debt to help finance the purchase. In our case, the direct costs we should have to receive when purchasing commercial property include: That gives us total annual recurring expenditures of $ 43,235.64. To extrapolate the annual recurring value at the 15-year time of the loan, we accepted the 2 percent annual rate of inflation, giving us overall recurring expenditures of $ 700,528.23 over the 15-year occupancy period. You will find our complete calculations in the program. Trade real estate investing- Commercial property investments mostly consist of business buildings. These leases will stay locked in for some years, resulting in the double-edged sword. When the trade property assets are fully leased with long-term tenants who held to richly priced contract charges, the income remains even if the contract charges on equal properties fall (provided the tenant doesn't go bankrupt). In contrast, the opposite is true-you might see yourself earning significantly below-market property taxes on the official business because you signed long-term leases before contract taxes increased.

The tax campaign bill that passed in December of 2017 was greater for trade property purchasers and agents than it was for those involved in residential property. Provisions favorable to commercial property believed to be in risk turned out being held. For example, Like-Kind Exchange principles even apply to property, but they were repealed for private possession.

After looking at some properties that are ready to rent, you might begin to wonder whether it is better to rent or buy the commercial property place. There are places when it might be better to get trade property instead of renting it. For example, if you purchase a commercial place, you can benefit from assets, income, depreciation, and asset appreciation. Getting tenants for technical properties is trickier. These assets attributes are leased for longer periods; Thus, commercial property investors must carefully choose tenants. Otherwise, when these attributes are empty, they tend to be empty for a time, which is something that no real estate investor desires.

There are numerous moving components involved in successfully renovating and establishing commercial property to the tenant's specifications. The best commercial property developers can control every aspect of the development process and work closely with tenants to create the place they want. Managing the trade property improvement on your own, in contrast, will quickly turn into time-consuming and costly without business experience. In contrast, the condition for commercial property investment is very different. Renters of commercial properties are the people who oversee compensating for many expenses including council taxes, insurance, property administration fees, etc. Therefore, the commercial property investor might just want to pay as little as 5 percent out of the rent had for expenses. This far increases the yearly rate of return on assets (JAMES CHEN, 2019)!

In contrast, not only does commercial property investing be a huge amount of assets but investing in technical properties (like business buildings and shopping malls) is a huge undertaking. That is why so many property investors shy away from trade property investment. Additionally, there exists a variety of technical property cases, e.g., business, marketing, office, and apartments, and let alone that within each place form there are numerous sub-types to choose from. For the experienced property investor, commercial property investment provides less completion and more chance to excel. Dolt shows his acclaimed technical real property semi- NAR planned to show you the ins and outs of investing at trade property. If you are investing in residential property or are begun to invest in trade property and need to get the investment to the next level, the way is for you. Identify these differences between advertising and residential property, and why advertising should take the next step for you.

Commercial property investment has been the hot-button issue in the property world, and there has been some discussion on whether it is better to spend in the trade or residential property. Those investing in residential properties have it is the least dangerous investment, while those fond of technical attributes contend that it is safer because of the income possibility. Dependent on the investment property, trade property investment will offer a higher guaranteed return on assets when compared to residential properties. As a summary, the mean ROI for trade properties ranges between 6–12 percent, while the median ROI for residential properties (like single-family houses) is typically just between 1–4 percent. As a result, trade property investment gives property investors the power to get more money every year, which can have a positive effect on the overall net worth (JAMES CHEN, 2019).

One of the primary reasons why you may spend in trade property at residential is the considerable earning potential. Commercial property properties normally take an annual return of the purchase value of between 6 percent to 12 percent (dependent on the country) which is much higher variety than typical returns for single-family properties (from 1% to 4% at best). When you purchase a commercial property, you will typically have to spend as much as six more at direct prices when compared to renting a commercial property. This is because most people who purchase commercial property business this purchase with the debt that needs up to at least 10-20 percent as the cut cost (but his number can easily climb to 40%).

When learning how to spend in trade property, do not leave about flipping. If you want to flip commercial property, this place needs to be either considerably undervalued in the moment of purchase or remodeled to change the amount enough to get a profit. Flipping is for the investor with enough money to get up the place and the power to take off while expecting the sale, since trading technical properties mostly do n' 't happen as quickly as selling a house. The average time it takes to be the commercial place in the hot market is relatively quick, while in the slow industry it would take years. There is one downside, yet. When it comes to being paid as the trade property agent, the downside lies in the length of this bargain. Trade property deals will more frequently than not be very time-consuming and complex. The average commercial property deal will go from six months up to the year too short – sometimes even longer, and sometimes the agreement does' 't still close.

2) Trade property: Commercial real estate requires investing in properties that are intended just for technical or business purposes. One example of investing in commercial property could be investing in the center, a local park or even a petrol station. Investing in commercial property often requires large initial capital and generally technical property agents could be needed to speed up the transaction.

In contrast, getting many assets in trade property investment is much easier as there are some financing choices to choose from. As a trade property investor, not only do you have the power to increase capital by using conventional funding choices, but you may also take the assistance of hedge funds, investment groups, and private equity firms. Commercial property investors will also pool assets and have access to more funding to buy the finance property. All states in the US need a license to permit you to be commercial property. This means that you as a commercial property agent would have to be certified by the government. Gaining a license for growing into a commercial property agent means that you want to give the written test. Additionally, Most states can also need potential agents to fill 30-90 minutes of different property classes (some may make you the example if you get a bachelor's level in real estate) which can be done online or through actual classroom courses (these could be taken at community colleges).

We spoke to experts in this field and put together the guide on how to take the commercial property license and make the business buying, marketing, and renting commercial real estate. While the way to trade property, nirvana is different for everyone, the guide can go through the core skills and training you will want to get started. Flipping commercial property represents the peak of the profitable business. If for nothing else, trade property is the physical business, one experiences after they have mastered residential property investment. That said, commercial property typically is not the initial exit strategy people prefer; rather, it is a thing they want to get towards. If you are interested in flipping commercial property, take reading the first two components of the series:

The successful commercial property investor has the potential to have a very profitable business. Some beginner investors have multifamily properties as the gateway to go into commercial property investment. Regardless, it is imperative that you get a specific business idea before getting started. Here are these responses to a couple of commonly asked commercial property questions every beginner investor should remember: Â€¢ Residential real estate markets and trade property markets are essentially distinct. Residential property is the production process that counts on consumers to buy new-made and existing products. Trade property is an investment activity that rents properties to businesses and consumers. Current technical properties are owned by investors and just made when there is enough current requirement (JAMES CHEN, 2019).

There are some conflicts between residential and technical property from legal, practical, and functional points of view, all of which, without example, give trade real estate a far superior investment. We talk about these differences in section 3. For today, I need to highlight the biggest fundamental- Tal change between residential and technical property. Philosophically, with residential property, you exist considering with

To understand why the property investment life should be focused on trade property, let us examine aspects of commercial property and residential real estate. The relation is a useful exercise in that most readers are likely familiar with this residential condition but not with the technical analog. I anticipate that some of the worlds of commercial property would be a surprise to you and a nice one in this. Let us start. If you were involved in growing into a trade property agent, then it would be best to gain some experience at the commercial property to get in this specific section in your target firm. However, certainly, residential property is most likely where the travel will be, as residential property is more suited for entry-level investors and brokers alike. However, you should always keep a clear view of the goal and take every chance to go up to commercial property after gaining some experience in residential property (JAMES CHEN, 2019).

Just like with commercial property, you should thoroughly evaluate the amount of and exchange for the residential property place before making the offer. With residential property, there are fewer neutral methods of assessment of property, particularly single-family residences. If the house is the multifamily component, examine an income that property generated in tandem with property taxes, and utilities. With single-family residences, comps, property appraisals, and local property trends are the best bet for respecting this place. Preserving that commercial place sometimes includes altering the exterior or interior of the business. If the windows and doors of these trade property places are outdated, not trendy, or poorly planned, consider updating them as that will change the show of the investment property, and thus increase its value. Furthermore, painting that right brick is another simple and easy way to modify the show of the commercial place without making great structural changes.

The reality of property investment is huge and has several types of investment properties for the property investor to choose from. There are single-family houses, multi-family houses, townhouses, trade property properties, etc. Naturally, each kind of investment property yields different income. Therefore, to make the best positive income investments, place investors want to investigate these various options. As summary, multi-family houses consist of more than one construction unit, however, managing the kind of finance properties generates lower prices per unit than single-family homes. When purchasing and selling commercial property, appraisers often rely on three established methods to determine the actual value of the place (JAMES CHEN, 2019). In societies, e.g., San Francisco, where commercial property is in high demand, the amount of commercial property has been pushed progressively higher alongside the personal property. Business owners and entrepreneurs who are, seeking out trade property to start their enterprises should be aware of these various arguments that impact property costs at their desired area.

Real Estate Trust

REIT stands for property Investment confidence. The real estate investment trust is just a company that owns and controls the income-producing property. People may spend in REITs through the stock exchange, as they are frequently publicly sold, and they enable the person to make a relatively small amount of money and spend in income-generating real estate. With the invention of property finance trusts in 1960, property ownership is the mouse-click out. REITs have an income-producing property in different spheres (JAMES CHEN, 2019). These investments are regulated by the Securities and commerce Commission, business on better product exchanges and pay daily dividends. REITs are required by force to give out 90% of their income at dividends. Beyond REITs, there are many ways to have property, without purchasing the place.

Some speculate about how to make money at the property through huge investments like multiple houses, skyscrapers, malls, among others. This solution is property investment trusts or REITs. REITs are corporations that buy huge property investments, e.g., the ones just mentioned. What is important about REITs is that they are legally needed to assign 90 percent of its dividends to that related investors each year. On the flipside, nevertheless, these dividends are taxed as common income, which may be the matter if you are at the higher bracket. Take commercial property. Publicly named property Investment Trusts (REITs) offer some liquidity, but they are costly to make up and typically take a container of properties rather than a single business. Moreover, REITs are typically purchased and take vehicles, so most investors are kept out of development tasks altogether unless they will provide minimums which are much on the request of $ 25k and higher. One time you might be able to purchase $ 10 of the single trade property asset like the Empire State business or spend $ 100 in the process of the LEED-certified housing project. Tokenization can make IRS 1031 exchanges simple.

Property investment trusts (REITs), which started when the property investment Trust Act turned into effective on New Year's Day, 1961, are free. REITs, like savings and debt associations, are dedicated to property lending and may and do provide the domestic property industry, although some specialization has happened in their activities. REITs the property investment trust, or REIT, is the corporation that owns or finances the income-producing property. REITs may be corporations, small liability companies, or enterprise trusts (some states have statutes making property finance trust entities). Although REITs routinely have institutional investor owners, REITs were made to assist investments by people together at institutional-quality property assets without the people having to immediately develop and accomplish the real estate assets.

Another investment strategy for giving money at the property without purchasing finance property is by investing the money in property investment trusts. REITs were presented in 1960 for the aim of giving investors the power to invest in property as the asset, without the necessity for purchasing finance property. REITs just need assets from their investors. Thus, property investors get shares of this REIT, while property ownership belongs to the REIT, which divides the gains in exchange for the assets.

REIT stands for the Property Investment Trust. In the simplest definition, the REIT is to the property place as mutual money equals to the product. A great number of people pool their funds together, forming the REIT, and permit the REIT to buy huge property investments, e.g., shopping malls, huge housing complexes, skyscrapers, or bulk amounts of single-family homes. This REIT then distributes incomes to various investors. This is one of the most hands-off ways to invest in property but does not have that returns seen in hands-on investment. This REIT idea was established in Australia in 1971. Chief Property confidence was the early Australian Property assets trust (LPT) on the Australian stock exchanges (today the Australian security Exchange). REITs that are listed on the commerce were called named Property Trusts (LPTs) until March 2008, differentiating them from personal REITs, which are recognized at a country as Unlisted Property Trusts. They have since been renamed Australian property finance Trusts (A-REITs) in connection with global training (JAMES CHEN, 2019).

The property investment trust (REIT) is a corporation that owns or finances income-making property. They make like to stock investments by providing general shares to the people but are uncertain about the government of the property industry rather than on the exchange. Essentially, REITs are part of the personal and national interest fund at property corporations that invest in properties, mortgages, and other serious estate-related investments— and they offer all types of regular income streams, diversification, and long-term assets understanding. Real estate â€" Real estate investments comprise of property finance trusts, place funds, and restricted partnerships. Property investment trusts are classified as tier 1 and are valued from quoted exchange costs. Property funds are classified as either grade 2 or point 3 depending upon whether liquidity is set or there are some noticeable exchange participant dealings. Property funds are valued from third party estimates. Special partnerships are valued based upon evaluations offered by the common partners of these funds.

(b) The property investment trust represents the ownership interest in the personal equity fund. The property assets trust invests in the varied portfolio of mainly institutional-quality property assets within the United States. This money has the long-term investment goal of delivering the 8-10 percent overall return at the market cycle. All portfolio assets are developed through Clarion Lion

Properties Fund property, L.P., a small business. These attributes within this portfolio are valued every quarter to establish exchange worth estimates of the money's assets to demonstrate the stock's net asset worth.

I believe the asset courses that create this most income in these national markets are: Student set partnerships (MLPs), property finance trusts (REITs), mortgage real estate investment trusts (m-REITs) and business development companies (BDCs). Putting in all four of these investments simultaneously, can aid support diversification and low portfolio risk? The property investment trust, or REIT (said `` REET "), is the investment vehicle that pools investor wealth to purchase property assets. Remember the REIT as related to the exchange-traded stock, or ETF, except instead of investing in stocks or bonds, the REIT uses investors' wealth to develop properties. Broadly speaking, most people have the term `` REIT " when relating to interest REITs, and for the end of the section, you may expect that I am speaking about equity REITs unless I specify otherwise. Mortgage REITs represent a quite different kind of finance -- in fact; they are not yet included in the S&P's property sector

Investors in search of manageable income from property may need to take property investor confidence or REIT. The REIT is a corporation that buys, sells, produces, and manages the property, e.g., office buildings, housing complexes, shopping malls, self-storage units, and construction developments. Successful REITs will give investors higher yields, new income, and modest growth. The REIT (property Investment Trust) is a mutual fund that aggregates property properties (apartment buildings, trade structures, leisure properties, etc.). For the fee, professionals oversee these properties, take rent, and pay expenses, and you get the remaining income. As part of a varied portfolio, REITs will be a great retirement investment option (JAMES CHEN, 2019).

Property finance trusts (REITs). These are a thing like property-shared funds that put in real estate or property mortgages. You get shares at the REIT, so take income through dividends and/or capital appreciation. There are also important taxation rewards for REITs. It will be a clean investment if you do not need to get your hands dirty and seek to decrease the risk. REITs stand for property Investment confidence. This implies that investing in

REITs is like putting in property, albeit without place cooling methods like ABSD. As for any property assets, the macro attitude of the economy determines the returns of the assets. For REITs, there exist five sub-sectors: Business, marketing, Industrial, Hospitality, and care.

Stephen McKenna, the economics professor at the University of Oregon, writes: `` take trade property. Publicly named property Investment Trusts (REITs) offer some liquidity, but they are costly to make up and typically take a container of properties rather than a single business. Moreover, REITs are typically purchased and take vehicles, so most investors are kept out of development tasks altogether unless they will provide minimums which are much on the request of $ 25k and higher ''.

These two most familiar cases of property assets trust are equity REITs and mortgage REITs. Most assets REITs typically get the property that generates income. The number of income-producing attributes includes buying malls, apartments, office places and renting single-family houses. If the property investment trust owns some property cases, it is called a diversified REIT. REIT stands for property assets Trust and is a corporation that purchases, produces, manages and sells property assets. REITs allow participants to put in the professionally managed portfolio of property attributes. REITs do as pass-through entities; corporations can administer the number of income cash flows to investors without tax on the firm level (JAMES CHEN, 2019).

Mortgage REITs, or m-REITs, represent the little variation on the property investment trust. These companies concentrate on the place mortgages versus the current property. These are more of the business tool, though you are investing in the company. This m-REITs debt currency for mortgages. They likewise buy mortgages and mortgage-backed securities. They make income from that benefit they make on mortgage loans. Some m-REITs goose their returns by bringing an advantage. Since they get their money on the spread between what they get in and what they give in, they will also have the advantage to increase return. To qualify as a property investment trust, the corporation must meet specific limitations. The REIT must spend at least 75 percent of its total assets in property of different cases. It also must take at least 75 percent of its total income in the form of property income from either the actual place or mortgage involvement or property sales. Therefore, you have two possible cases of REITs: Interest REITs, which have property direct and pay tenants to hire, and mortgage REITs, which spend in securities supported by the mortgages that real estate buyers use to finance their purchases.

Property investment trusts (REITs) give tax-efficient exposure to the property industry. In this confidence point, REITs are tax-exempt provided they give in least 90 percent of their incomes to stockholders, while investors must give ordinary income tax on their dividends and on shares bought and sold. Nevertheless, REIT contributions are taxed only after they get back the portion of the assets used to finance property purchases and improvements. Therefore, investors may determine their tax liability for their REIT contributions or at some years avoid taxes completely. Pooling money with additional investors to purchase the property through extra tax-advantaged businesses exempt from organized taxes under most conditions. These jobs are called property Investment Trusts (REITs) and much can be developed just like any other product through the business account. There are still ETFs and shared funds that specialize at REITs (JAMES CHEN, 2019).

Current forces in crowdfunding realty have opened the door for portals like Peer Street to provide immediate property assets to investors. Unlike property investment trusts (REITs) which represent secondary investments in property funds, real estate crowdfunding is the direct investment at a place. Properties are professionally managed, but prices are generally lower than putting in REITs and those returns are equal with primary control. Some property finance organizations, e.g., property finance trusts (REITs) and some pension funds and Hedge funds, take huge enough capital reserves and finance schemes to allow 100% equity in the properties that they purchase. This minimizes the danger, which comes from the investment but also determines possible ROI.

Another form of indirect investment is the property investment trust (REIT) —a mutual fund of property properties. You get shares at this REIT, which may be privately held or publicly traded on the exchange. This

REIT is the money put in several technical properties. Some REITs specialize, reducing investments kinds of places, e.g., shopping malls, apartments, or leisure properties. Then there are these fantastic things called property Investment Trusts (REIT), which is mostly the corporation or group that employs in commercial/residential investments, property management, and finance. REITs represent what common funds exist for stocks. You are giving capital to the corporation who is pooling funds and applying it to act and get profit in the real estate business.

Captive property investment trusts (REITs) are related to those strategies above in that they try to make more material expenses for the organization. To make up the scheme, the firm first transfers all its property properties into the REIT (property investment trust). Principally the company of the corporation then owns the REIT. Land REITs. The `` REIT this the property Investment Trust. This corporation owns controls or finances income-producing property (Investopedia). To do as the REIT, the organization must comply with some rules, including giving back 90 percent of its taxable income to shareholders. For a very decent measure (less than $ 10 per share in some cases), you may have a little part of a very large landholding company. Normally (but not always), these REITs get money by leasing out the earth. A two of the larger publicly traded Land REITs are Land Partners (FPI) and Gladstone acres (farming) (JAMES CHEN, 2019). The REIT, or property Investment Trust, is the publicly traded organization that owns or finances the income-producing property. Modeled after shared funds, REITs are needed to administer at least 90% of their taxable income to stockholders yearly in this form of dividends. In addition, over the longer period, the overall returns of exchange-traded U.S. Assets REITs have mostly outpaced those of other U.S. Capitals. REIT investment is also widely utilized by investors as the device for broadening the overall investment portfolio since REITs are not directly correlated to stock exchange execution.

Real estate investments represent the important portion of property companies' asset properties and their primary source of income. For instance, property finance Trusts (REITs) in America are taken by force to take at least 75% of their possessions at the property, derive at least 95 percent of income from property, dividends, and interest, and give dividends of at least 90 per pence of assessable income. Rules in different countries are related. Thus, the assessment of these corporations should be essentially driven by the same elements as privately held buildings at the underlying property markets. Property is the example, and some business advisers suggest a 5% to 10% distribution toward property investment trusts in most portfolios. Still, REIT dividends are taxed as common income, so take them at tax-sheltered reports, such as 401 (k) programs and personal retirement accounts, to prevent the tax hit.

These other sections have different measures that investors and analysts must measure the well-being of the real estate industry. All three segments have publicly traded property assets trusts, or REITs, portfolios of properties whose stock prices investors often must define and analyze business trends. Prologist (NYSE: PLD), Rexford Business (NYSE: REXR) and postscript enterprise stadium (NYSE: PSB) represent some of this most well-known REITs at this industrial real estate segment. The market brings together several property business participants, e.g., agents, surveyors for due diligence and money managers. This structure makes tools to support managers or corporations like REIT's (property Investment Trusts) to create national portfolios. Users who may not get specialized business knowledge will put in the managed portfolios that have produced the proven record of accomplishment for profitably. A similar idea has been applied on websites like Toro (JAMES CHEN, 2019).

Conclusion

As for trade property investment, in contrast, demand is not equally high. Not everybody wants to have the shop, and businesses do not go as regularly as people do. The commercial place is just up in great need in countries with profitable and business development. Furthermore, some property investors are not familiar with these policies about investing in a commercial place. Some beginner property investors are attracted to the commercial property industry. Yet, if you do not have the required knowledge or are in the environment at which demand is low, do not invest in technical attributes (JAMES CHEN, 2019)!

Car 343 property payments: two the way covers the basics of property and introduces students to real estate terminology. It talks about types of property, related legal issues involved in having property, and real estate contracts. This way also explains the advantages of having property, too as the requirements to be licensed to deliver property. Offered season. Requirements: ACC 216; junior position or above. Not the prerequisite for a successful business in property management is highly recommended. Some colleges and universities offer property and property management classes, increasingly offering points in property, and few offer points in place management. In addition, a college diploma or a graduate degree in business management or economics will offer a significant educational education in this area.

Real Estate* Our property education would enable you to develop a comprehensive understanding of property and the skills to make important decisions in place terms, property management and investing, and commercial property practice. You would have the chance to initiate research for the business customer, as well as the opportunity to ensure a useful job position. This way encourages studying through real-life tasks and scenario-based case studies. You can gain a detailed understanding of property, alongside the expert investigation of the processes of its relation, growth, job, evaluation, and governance. The user–friendly interactive class borrows from issues covered in a presentation to Commercial Property marketing and Property Management and Managing Risk. Issues explored include the nature of the commercial property, classifications of actual property, contract cases, exchange value, and rate of return analysis. The common name offers an up-to-date introduction to place management with a useful emphasis on how to comply with rules and prevent liability.

One example of a smaller cost way is the Introduction to trade property marketing which is perfect for anyone who may be interested in this potentially profitable area of trade property. The way consists of web-based language modules designed for computer or smartphone education. This matter ranges from identifying property cases and investment opportunities to developing a functional marketing program. The common continuing training elective offers a complete introduction to the potentially profitable area of trade property. In the way, you can see how to recognize the investment opportunity for different categories of commercial property, including business, retail, industrial, and multi-unit residential. You can also investigate the business and tax components involved in trade property. The elective features teaching aims and key statements and case studies to teach important concepts.

The basic class provides a comprehensive overview of the basics of commercial property and how it differs from residential property. Students will be able to identify and understand the broker's character and learn the various types of technical attributes, policies, evaluation methods, marketing and resources for more education. While it cannot provide an agent with the required tools to learn commercial property, it can inform the business and give some of the resources required to pursue the commercial transaction or a career in commercial real estate.
*****Available room only***** Certainly, to get the positive income from renting out residential properties, you have to keep the property place easily and to consider some matters, first the position of these property investments and target tenants. These two elements help ensure that this residential place stays occupied and yields positive income. For instance, if you have a residential place in the school

district area, you should spend in single-family houses, and the target tenants could be families.

That is the first reason why most people prefer to spend on residential attributes. With the right position and the good tenant, property investors will be securing passive income for some years before they get to sell the property place for the profit. While gaining property income every month, the residential property investor is also establishing property understanding of residential properties, implying that the amount of these property investments increases with each passing day. Successful property investors usually do the property industry investigation before making the investment decision to purchase the income place in the specific property industry. The property industry analysis assesses various locations and property markets considering all the factors mentioned above to get the best place to purchase an investment property. Furthermore, the property industry analysis also examines the income property itself and calculates its expected rate of return before making the purchase (JAMES CHEN, 2019)!

The beginning of how to invest in property is finding the property place to put in. There are more sources to make investment properties on the market, and using a variety of these resources, property investors have greater chances of getting the greatest investment place. Some of the greatest choices for getting investment properties on the market include the product list Service (MLS), networking, property auctions, and heat maps. The main reason people follow the property investment business is, certainly, the numerous financial advantages it must provide for property investors. While both single-family and multi-family houses offer the property investor with supportive income at this form of property income, single-family property investors have the power to get money from their investment properties through a different form: Appreciation (JAMES CHEN, 2019)! That is another reason why they are one of those greatest longer-term investments.

Web Resources

Chen, J. (2019). ALTERNATIVE INVESTMENTS REAL ESTATE INVESTING. Retrieved from: https://www.investopedia.com/terms/r/realestate.asp. Wikipedia.org (2019). Estate (land)-Wikipedia. Retrieved from: https://en.wikipedia.org/wiki/Estate(land).

Chen, J. (2019). REAL ESTATE INVESTMENT TRUST- REIT DEFINITION. RETRIEVED FROM:HTTPS://WWW.INVESTOPEDIA.COM/TERMS/R/REIT.ASP.

Chen, J. (2019). Homeowners Association- HOA Definition. Retrieved from: https://www.investopedia.com/terms/h/hoa.asp.

ForSaleByOwner.com, (2019). How Much Is My House Worth? | Get Estimated Market Value and Comps. Retrieved from: https://www.forsalebyowner.com/sell-my-house/pricingscout/.

IDXCentral.com, (2019). About IDXCentral.com- Real Estate Website Design and IDX Solutions Development. Retrieved from: https://www.idxcentral.com/about-us.cfm.

Bortz, D. (2019). Real Estate Agent, Broker, Realtor: What's the Difference? Retrieved from: https://www.realtor.com/advice/buy/whats-difference-real-estate-salesperson-broker/.

Kapre.com, (2019). Real Estate Career Advice Articles | Kaplan Real Estate Education. Retrieved from: https://www.kapre.com/resources/

www.ingramcontent.com/pod-product-compliance
Lightning Source LLC
Chambersburg PA
CBHW030007190526
45157CB00014B/1013